BIG XXL
Preschool Workbook
AGE 3 TO 5

222+ Activities Letter Tracing
Number 1-10 - Early Math
Coloring for Kids
Lines and Shapes Pen Control
Toddler Learning and More
Pre K to Kindergarten

Abby Lyon

THIS BOOK BELONGS TO:

_____

„I hear and I forget.

I see and I remember.

I do and I understand"

Confucius

Did you like this book and did it meet your expectations?
If you are happy with your purchase and brought joy to your child, I would be very
happy to receive a review on Amazon.

Feedback and reviews on Amazon are very important to me and my work as an author and educator. On the one hand I get feedback, I know what is well received and what is not.
On the other hand reviews help all the other customers too.

Just log into your Amazon account,select this book and let me know what you and your child think about it. With a little effort you would help me and all my other customers tremendously.
Thank you!

Abby Lyon

Table of contents

Instructions

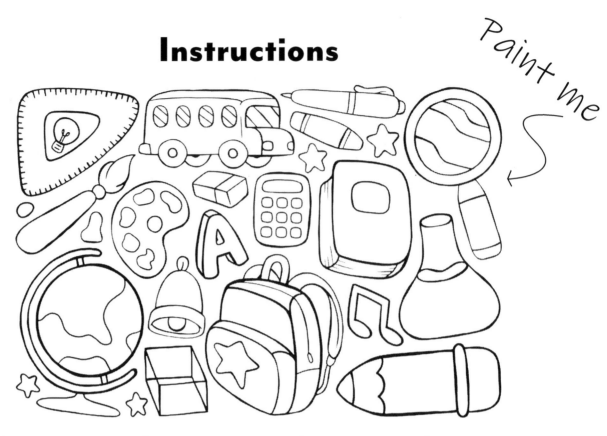

Paint me

We are about to start learning new things together.
But beforehand, I'd like to give you some tips and tricks along the way. With their help, you will get the most out of this interactive textbook.

The book is divided into several levels that we call stations: We will learn as we go along. So let's start at the first station and slowly work our way up until we reach the 9th station, the highest one.
Each level covers different topics and you always learn something new. For each exercise you will find many different images that you can color in. This keeps learning exciting and colorful.

To learn and practice in the best way possible,
we`ve got some tips for you:

1. Choose a comfortable place to study. Make yourself comfortable and move way from all the distractions. When you begin with the exercises, all other toys should be out of reach and put away in order to concentrate better.

2. At the same time, prepare all the important materials you will need to solve the tasks: pencils, paints, crayons, etc.

3. Chose a period of time in which you want to study and try keeping it the same. A rhythm will help you learn in a better way. Divide your study sessions into rea-sonable parts and set deadlines that you will keep.

4. Practice makes perfect. By repeating what you've learned over and over again, you'll remember more easily new content.

5. Good sleep and exercise are important: our brain is part of our body and is important for studying. That's why a healthy and balanced sleep is very important for learning. Lots of exercise and fresh air relax body and mind.

6. Take breaks. If you have already worked hard today, you deserve a break and a small reward.

But now let's get down to work.

I hope you have fun learning, reading, writing, calculating and solving puzzles!

Together now we travel on our train from one station to the station, always learning new things.

Station 1: Tracing shapes and figures

Now we are ready to begin at the first station.

Before we start writing and calculating,
let's learn how to trace figures and shapes.

It's going to be a lot of fun.

Here you will find some images.
Trace the line that is drawn.

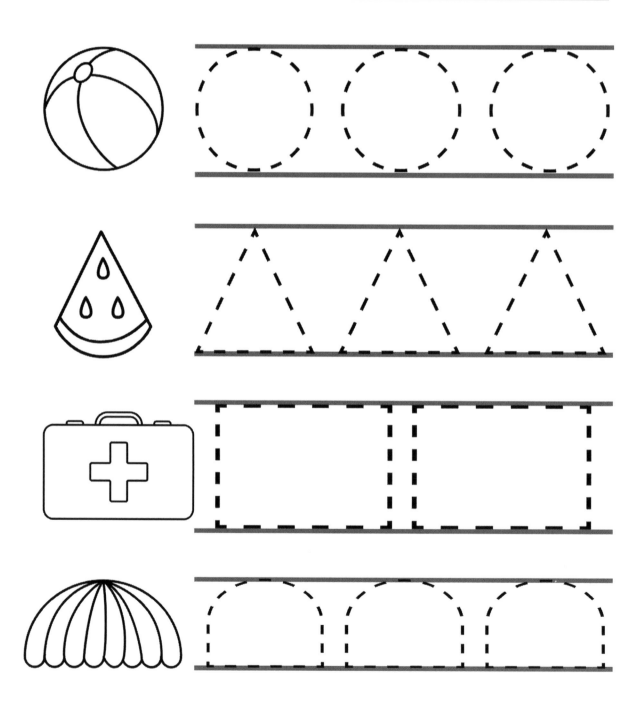

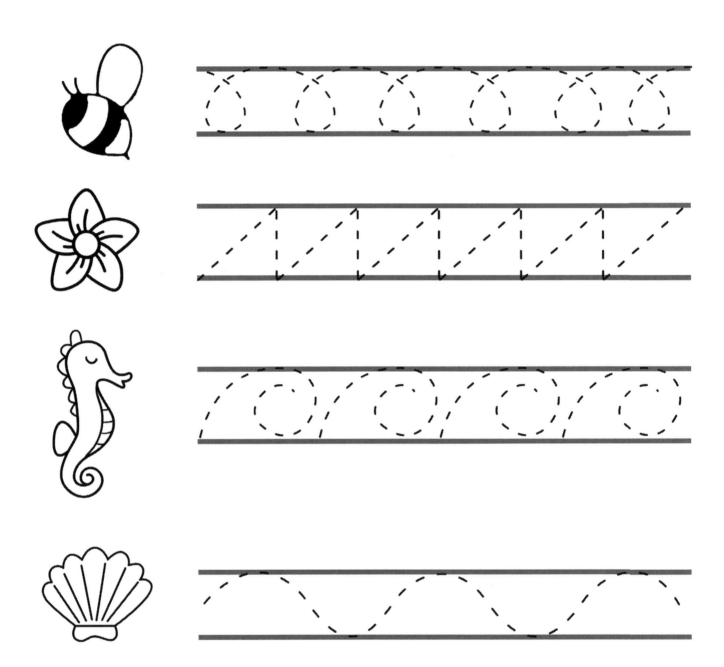

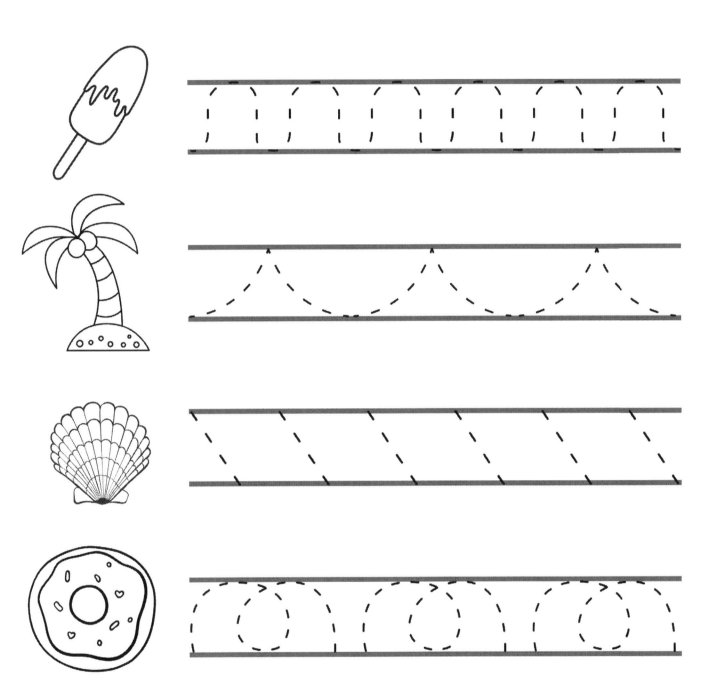

Draw the correct shape beneath the object.

Station 2: Learning the alphabet

Well done!
You have already made it to the second station!

In this station we are going to learn
the alphabet.
Chose your favourite pen and go
pass on from letter to letter.

Let's go!

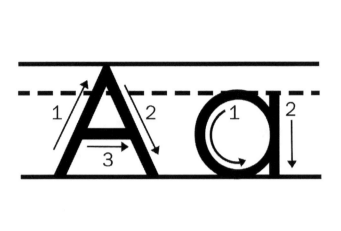

apple

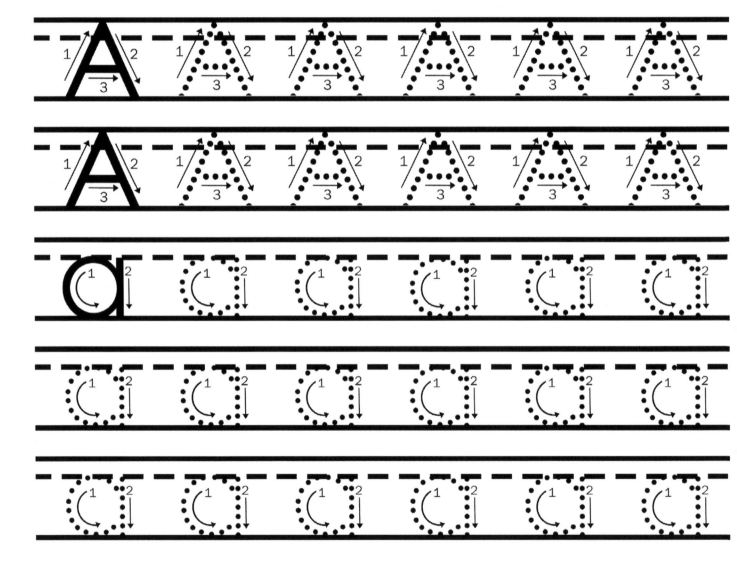

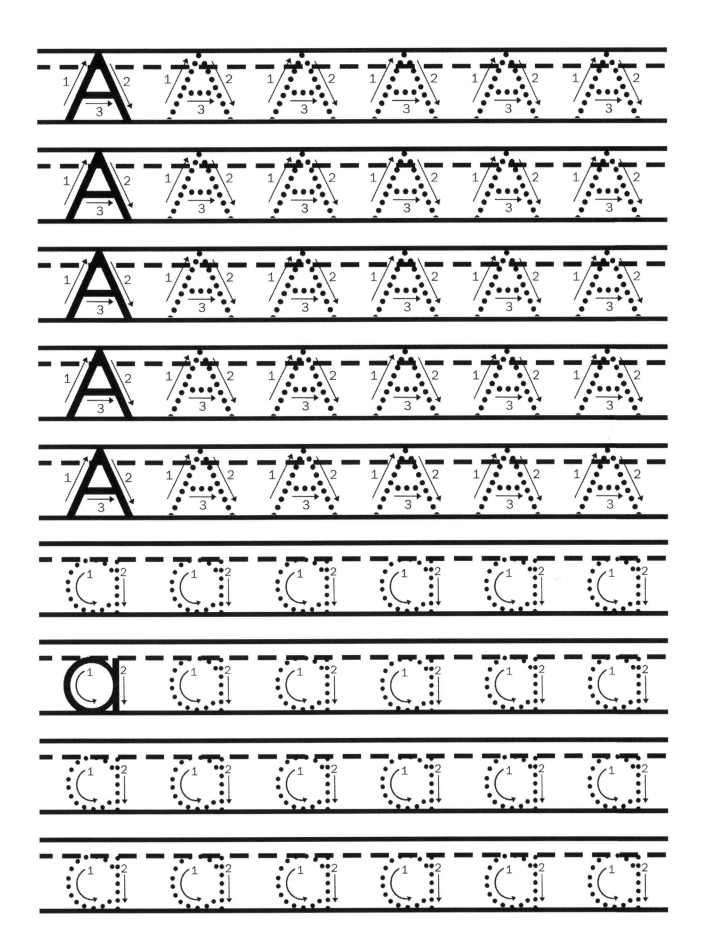

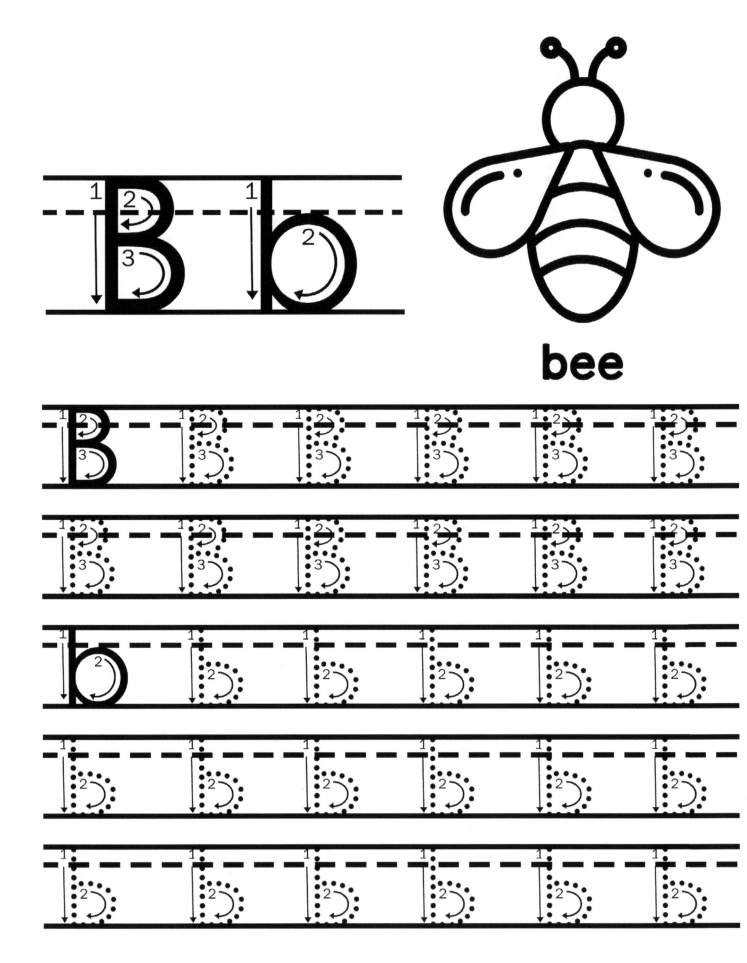

bee

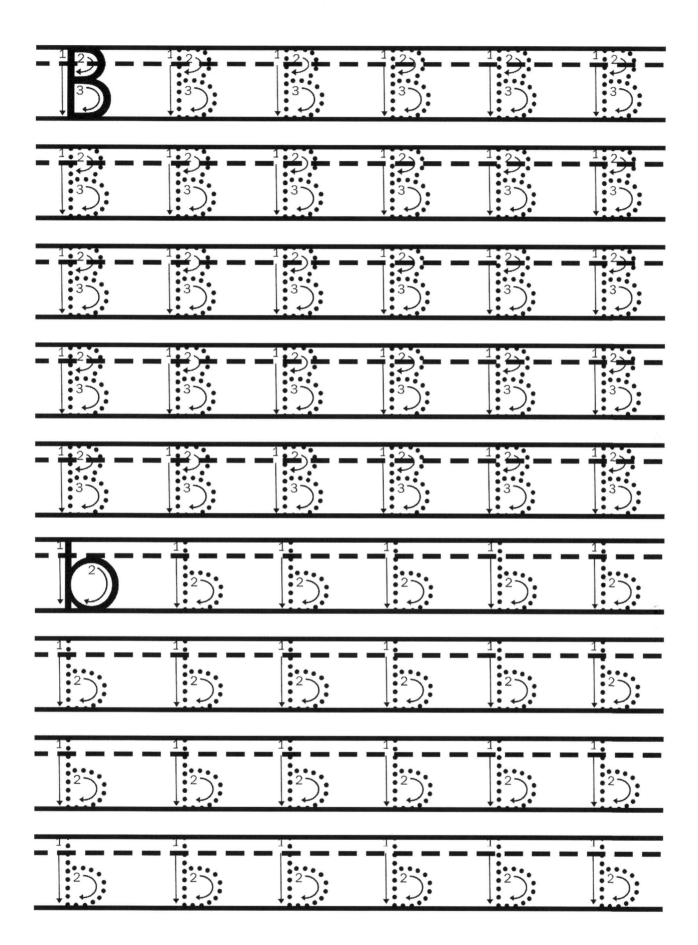

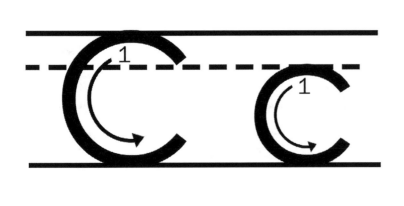

cat

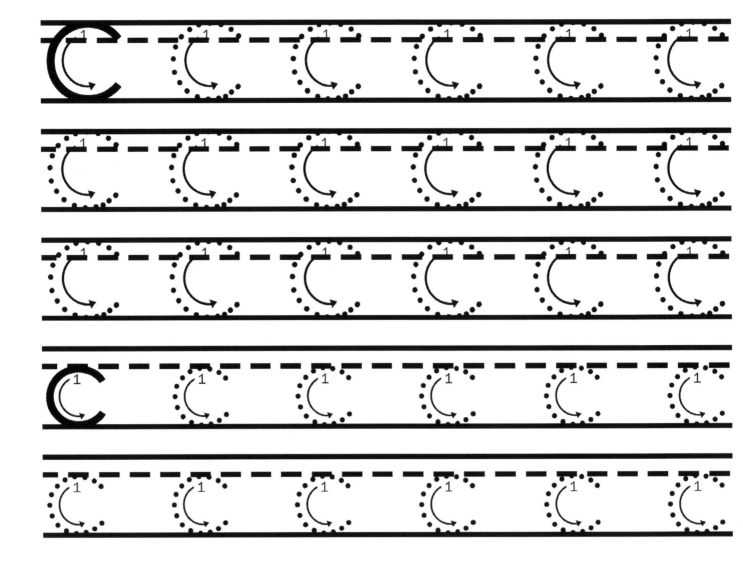

30

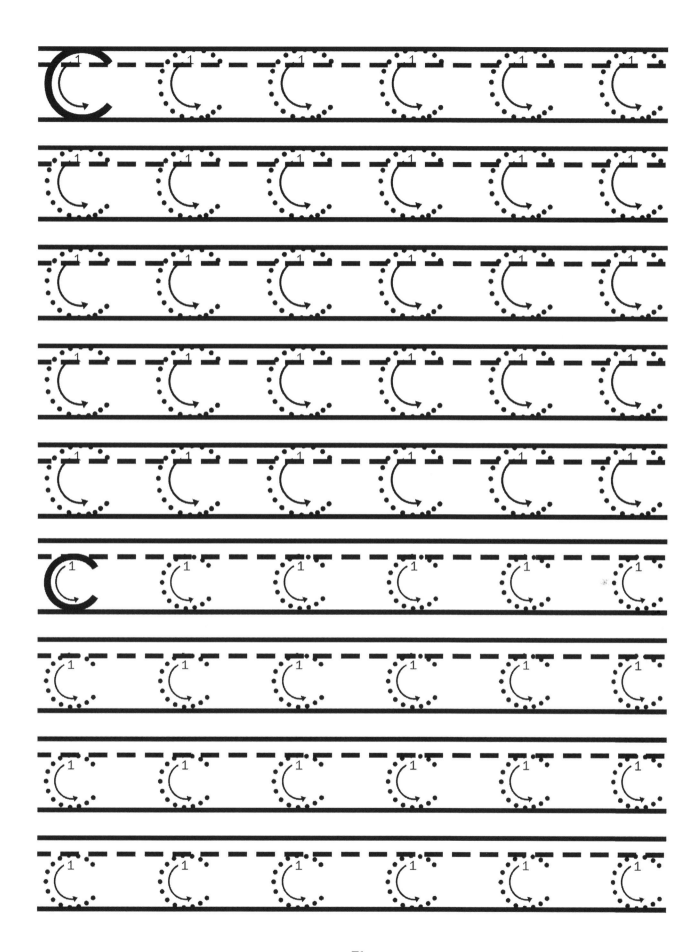

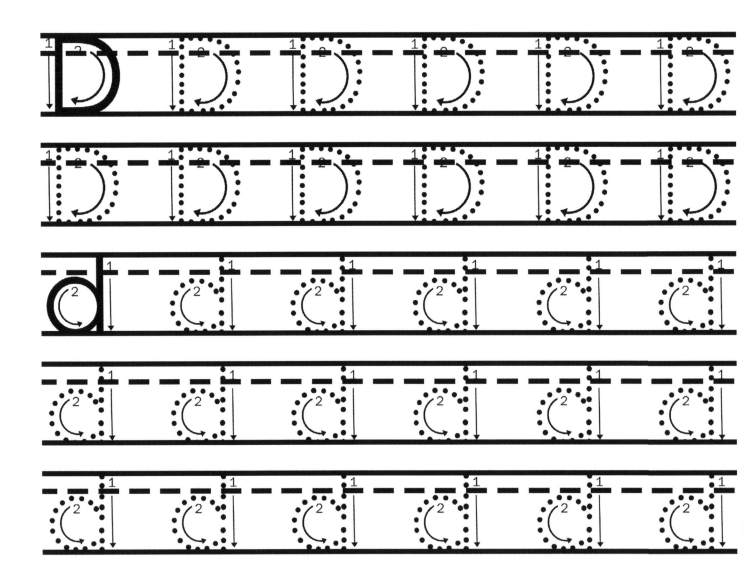

dog

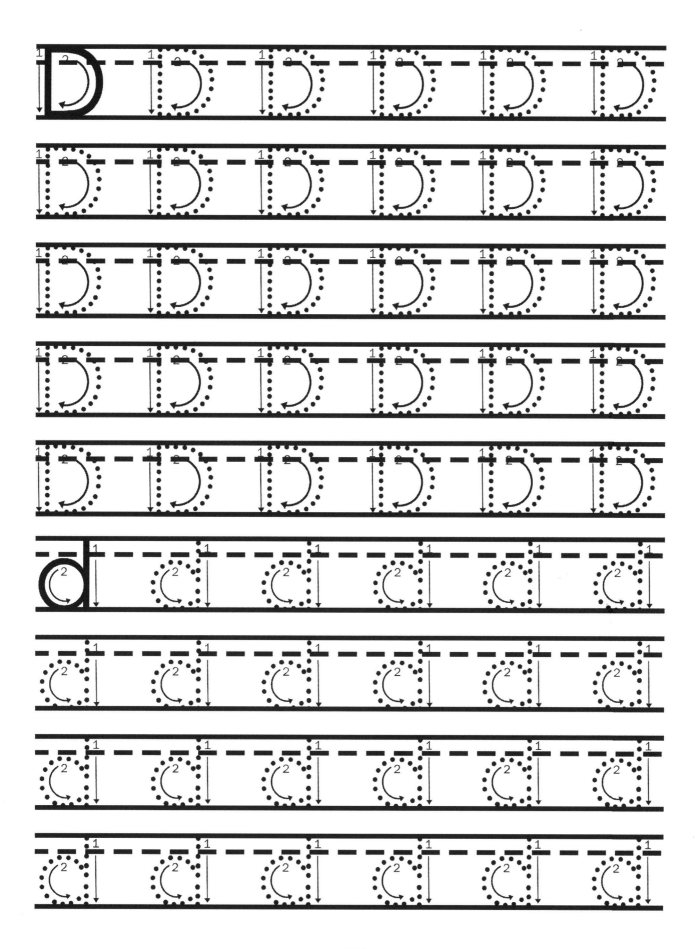

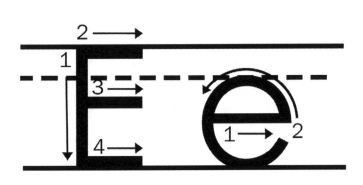

elephant

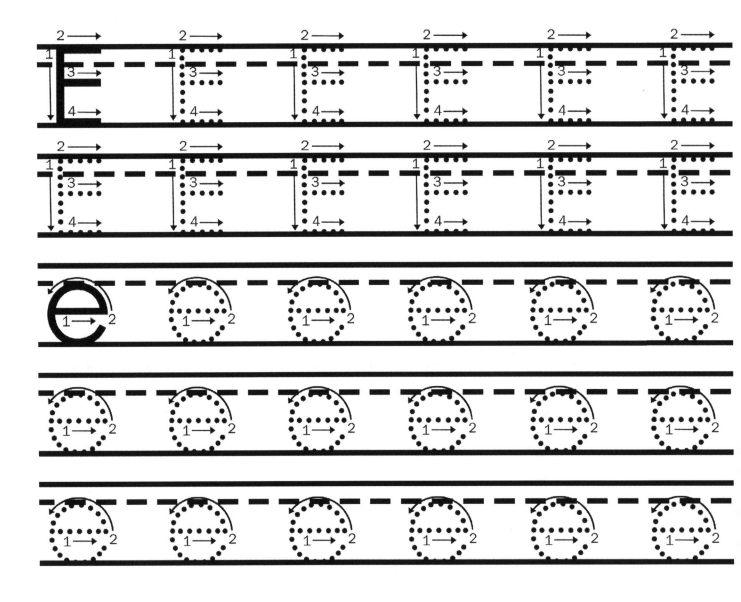

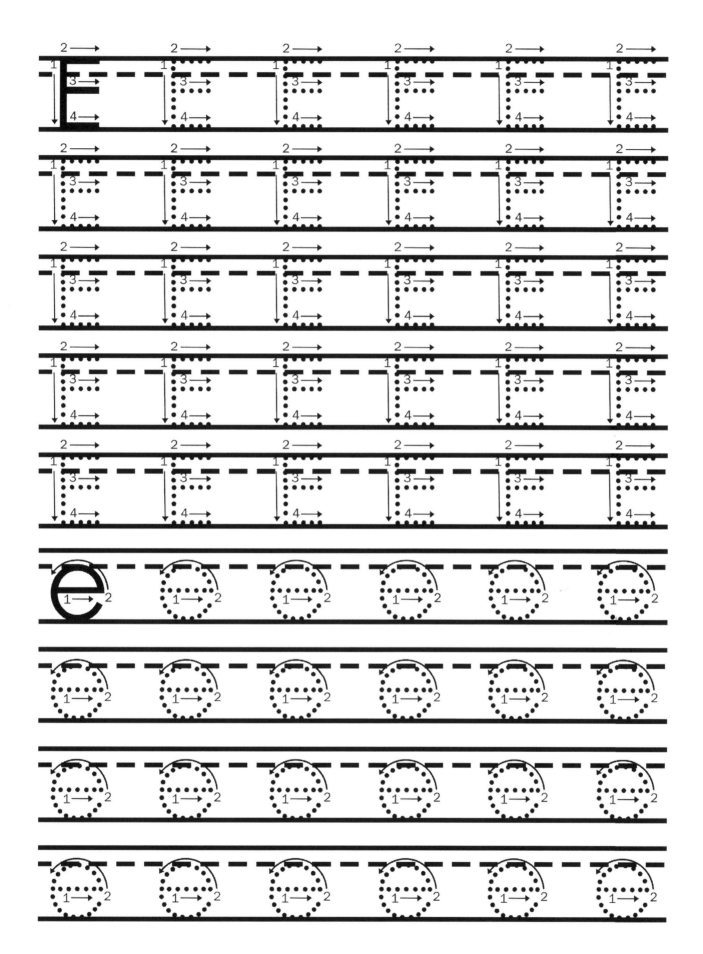

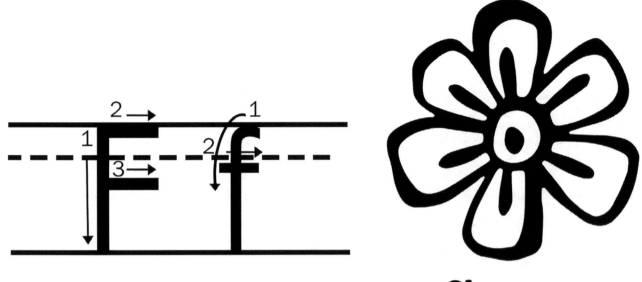

flower

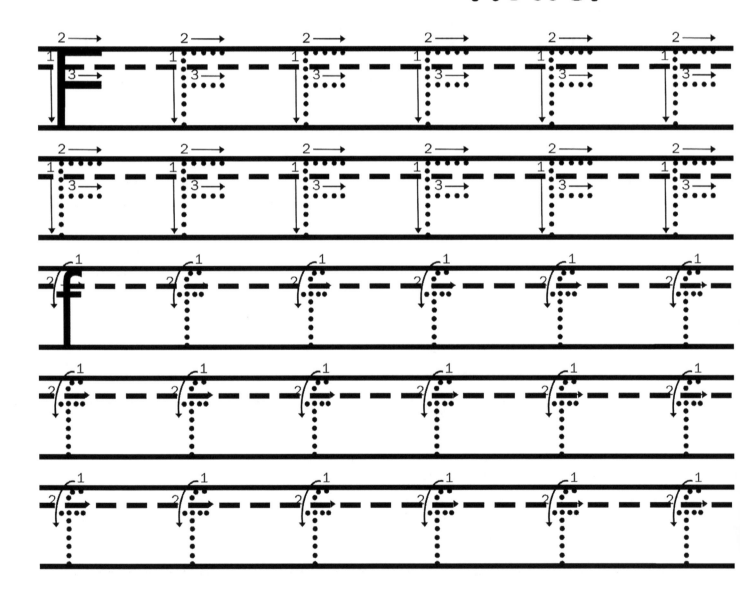

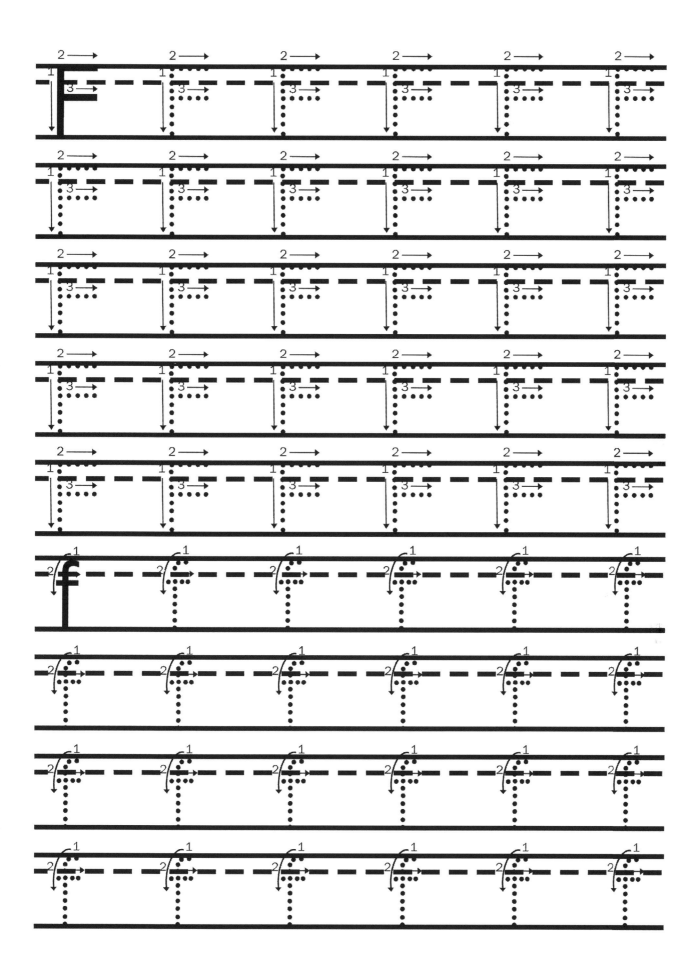

giraffe

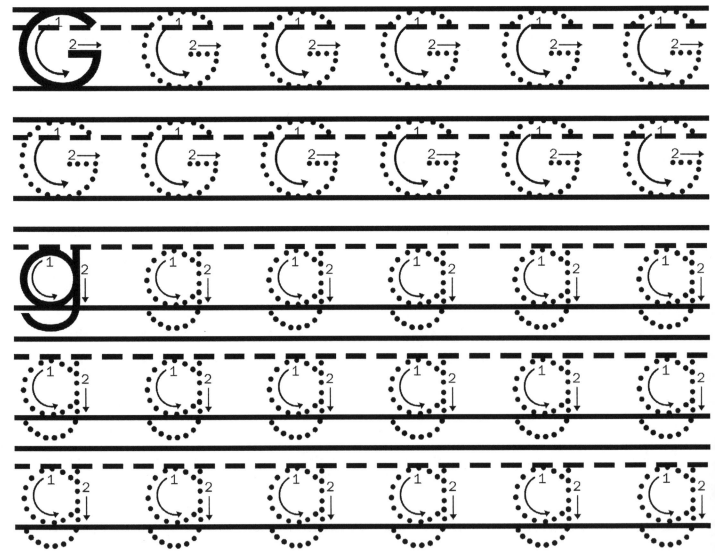

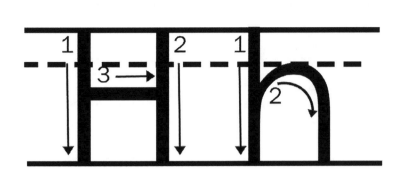

house

40

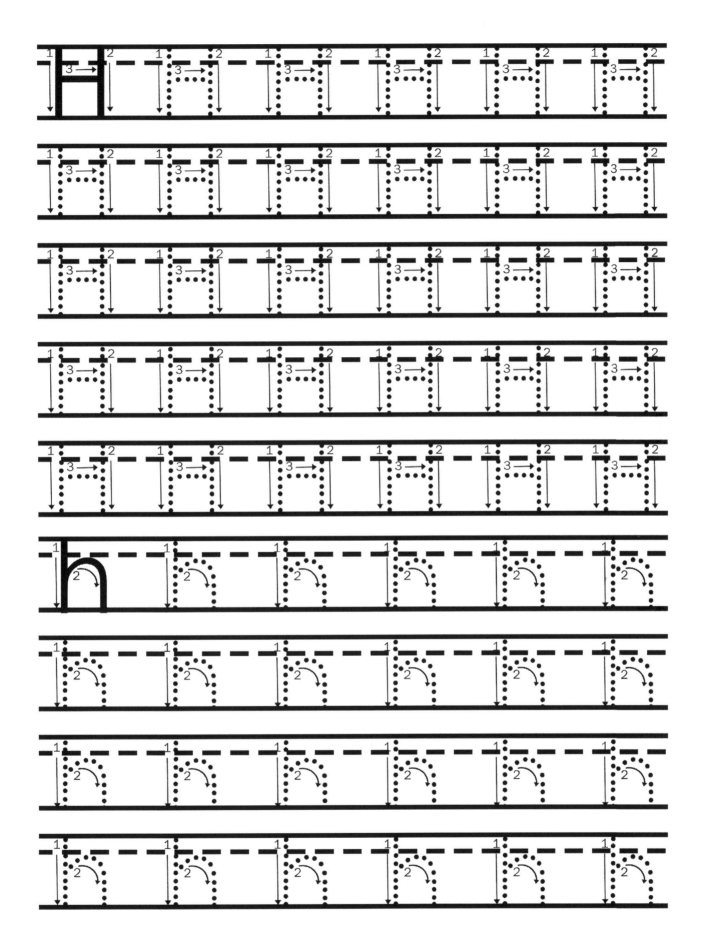

41

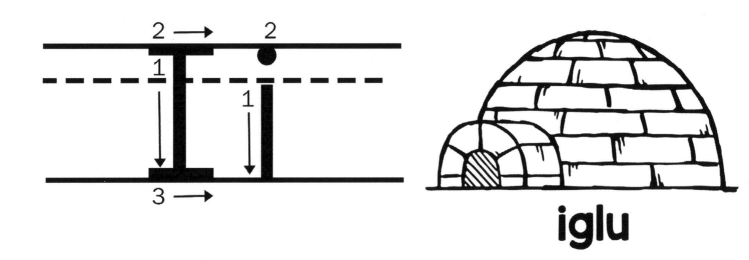

iglu

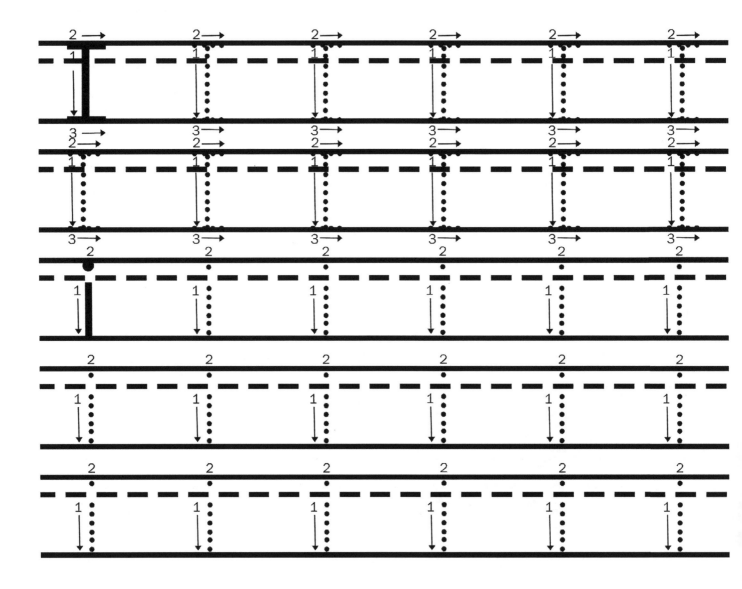

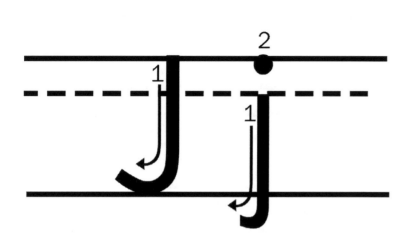

jellyfish

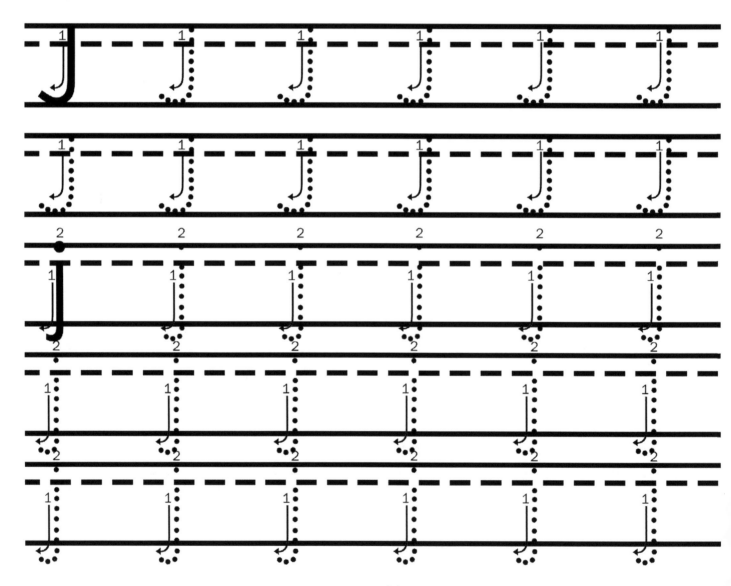

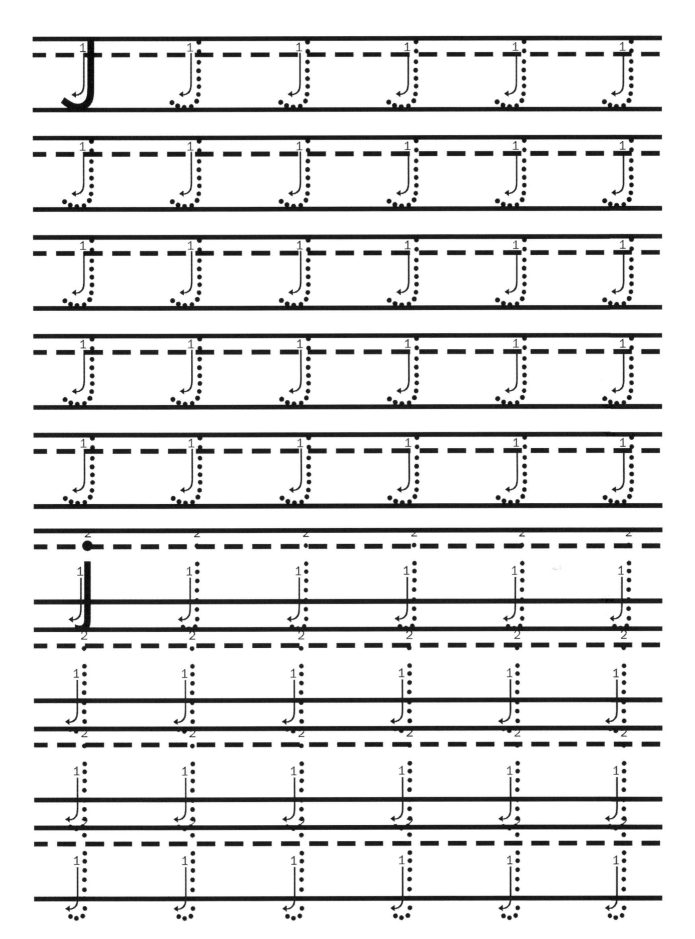

45

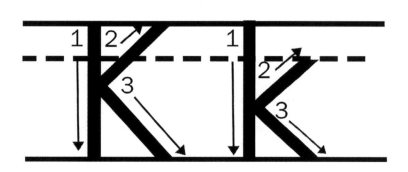

king

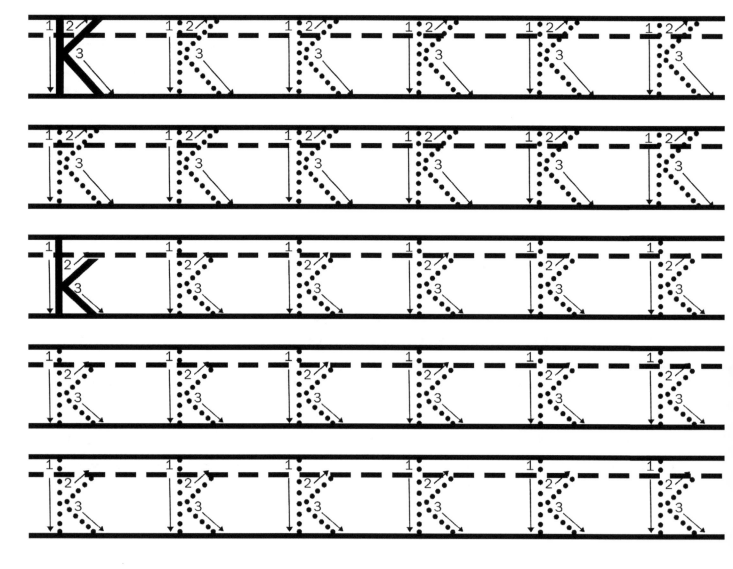

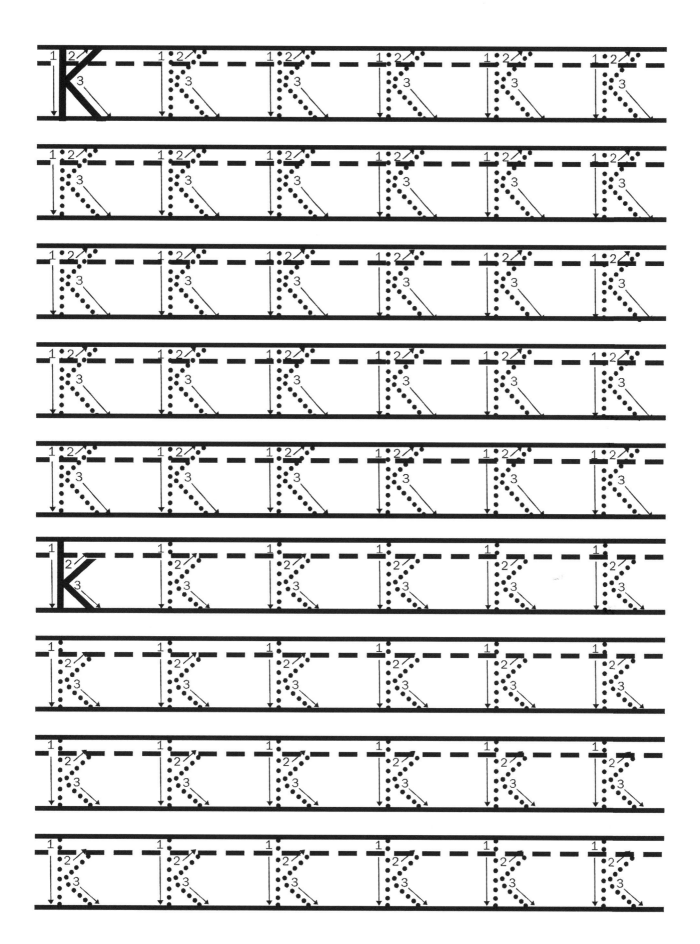

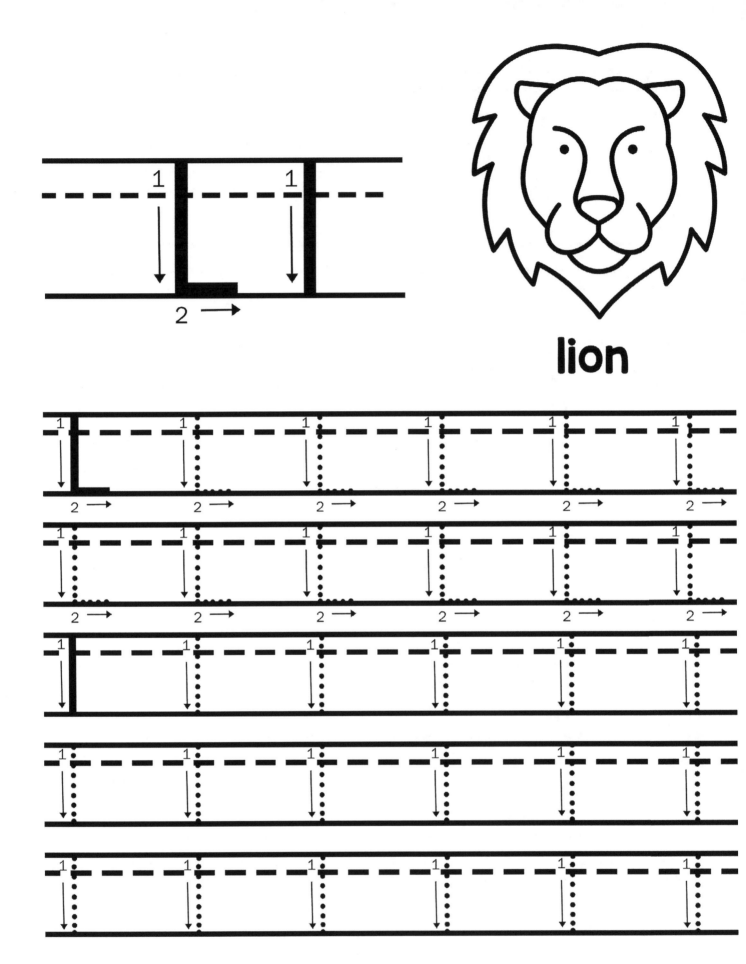

lion

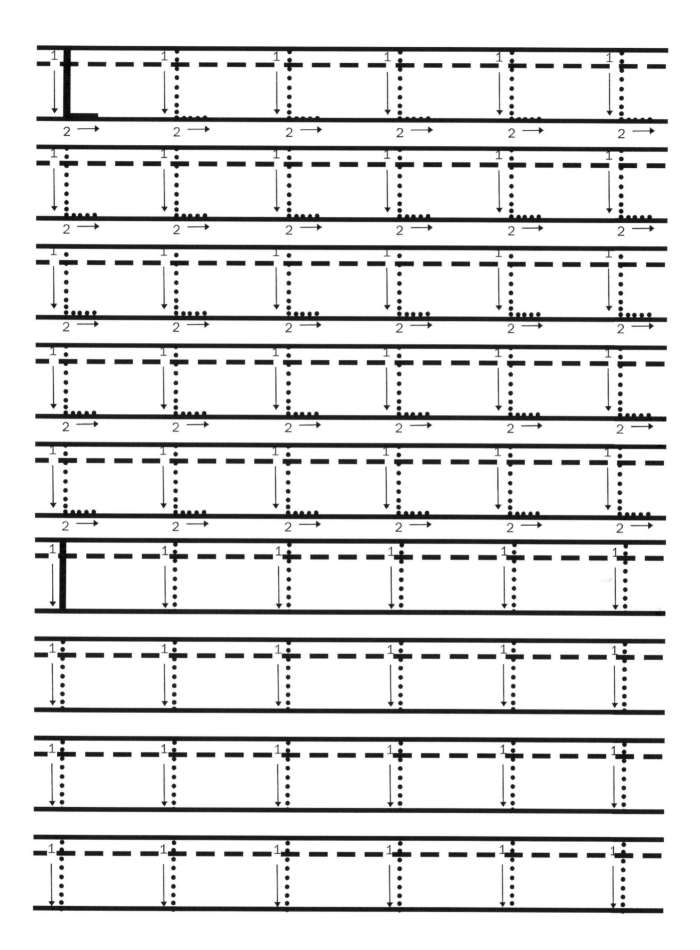

49

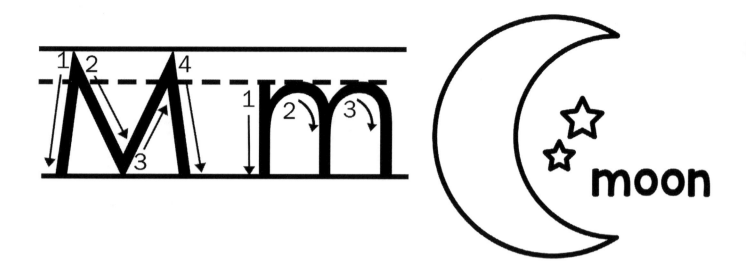

moon

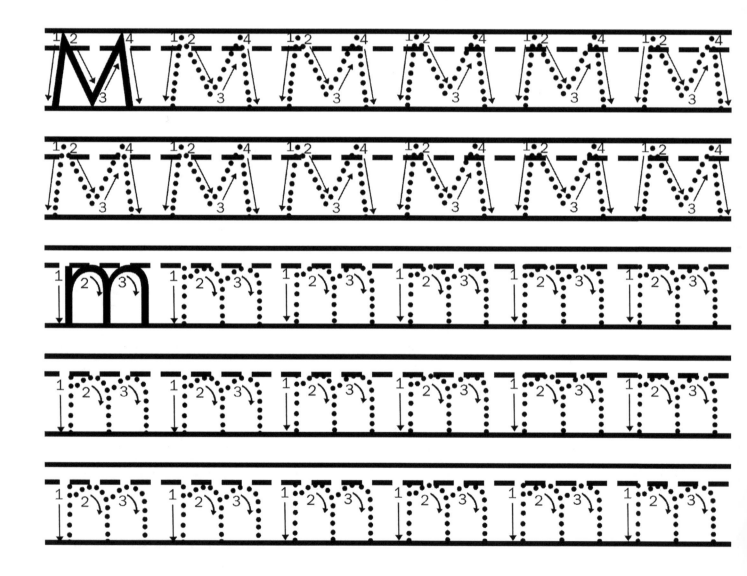

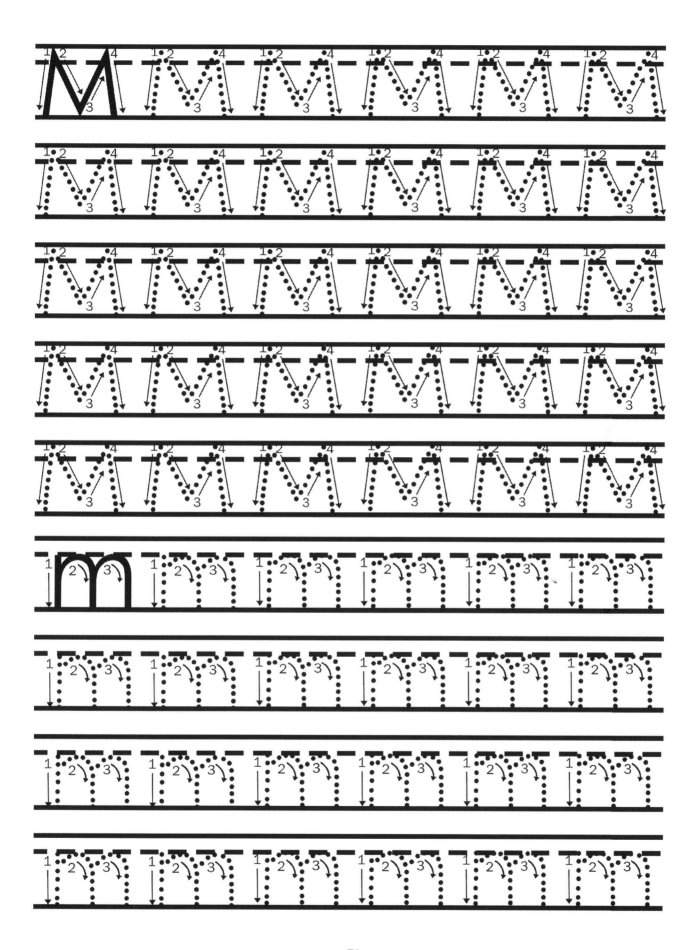

nest

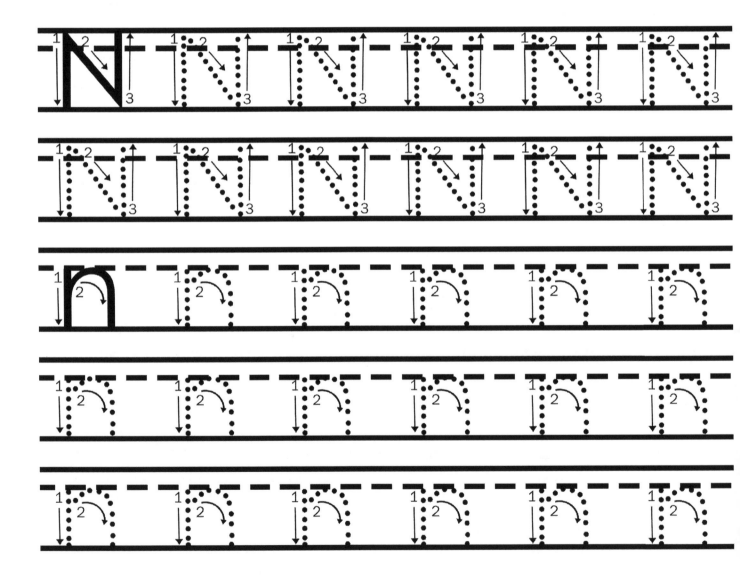

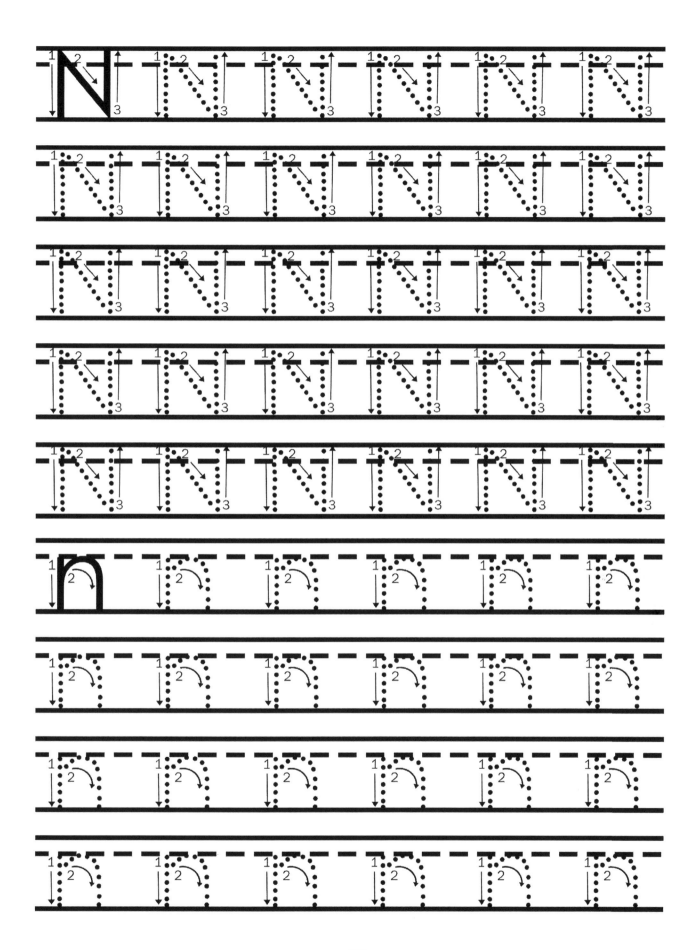

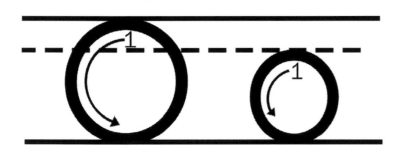

owl

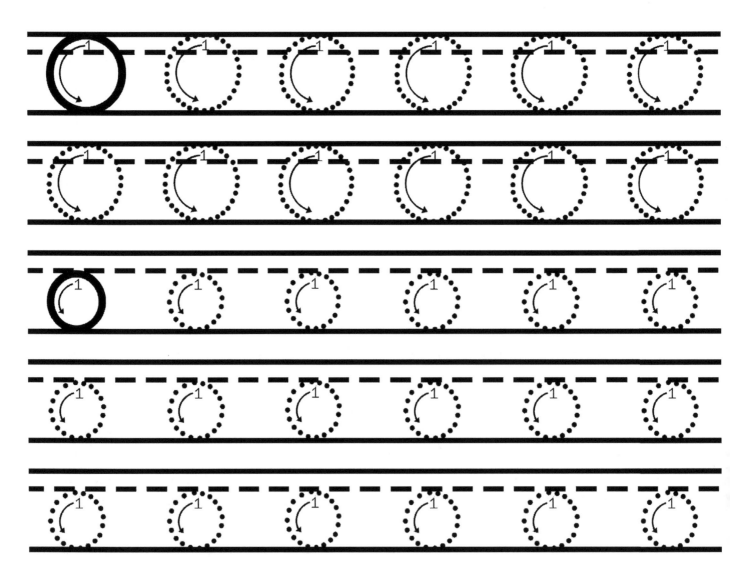

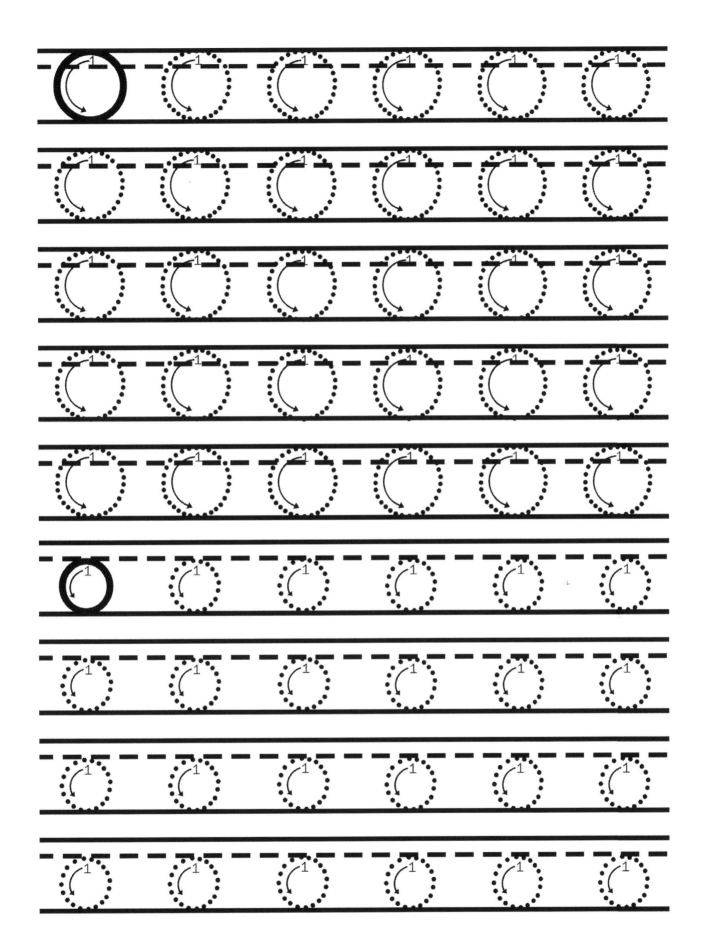

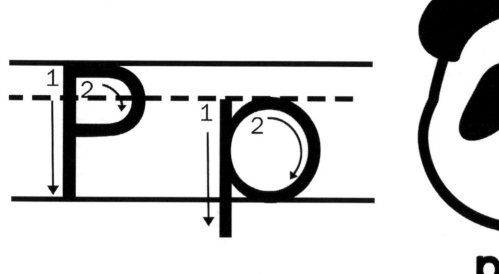

panda

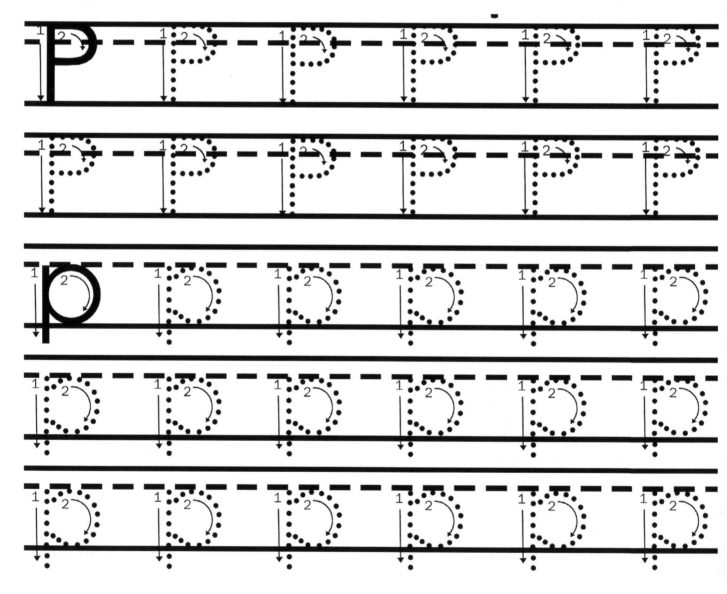

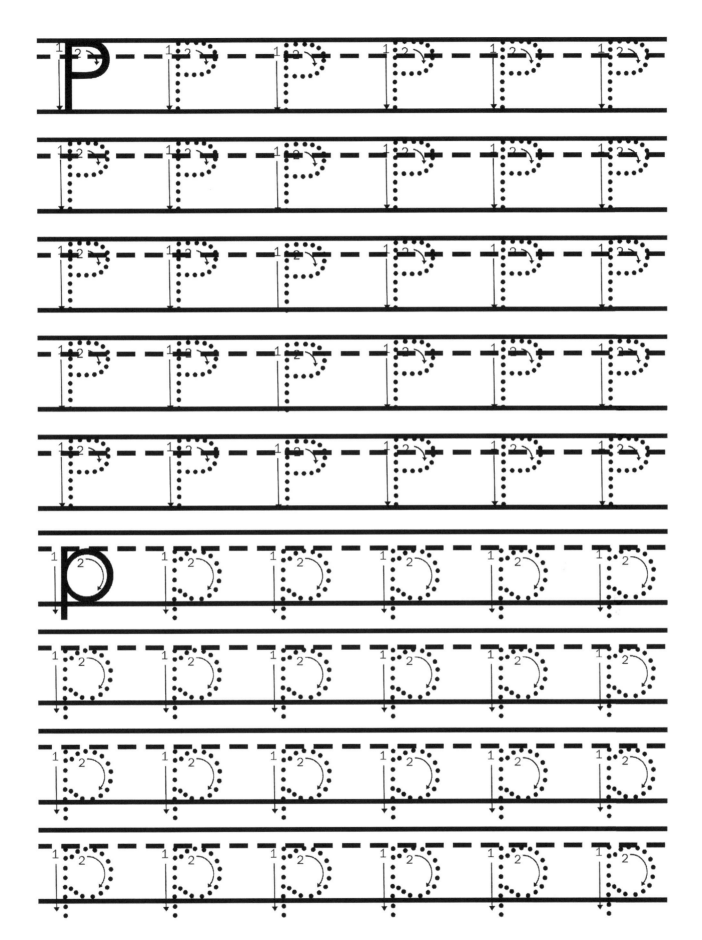

57

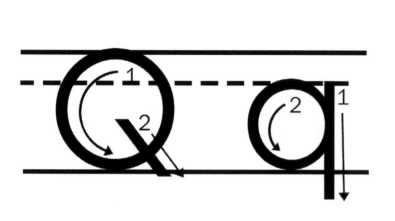

queen

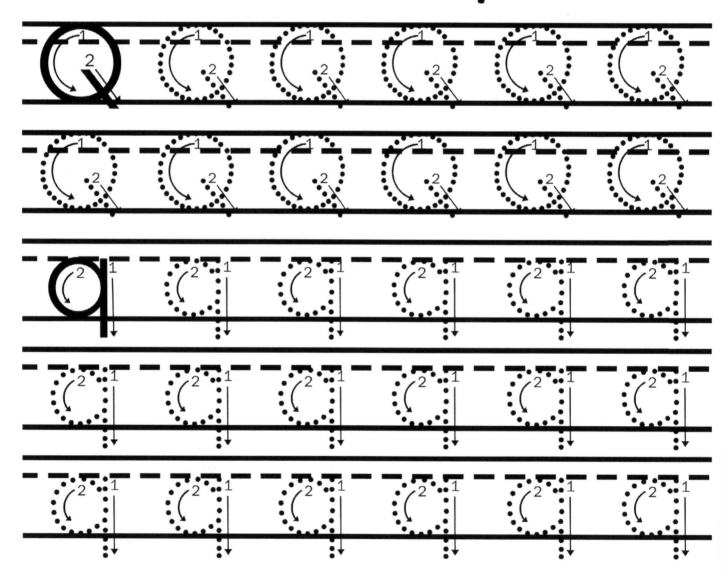

58

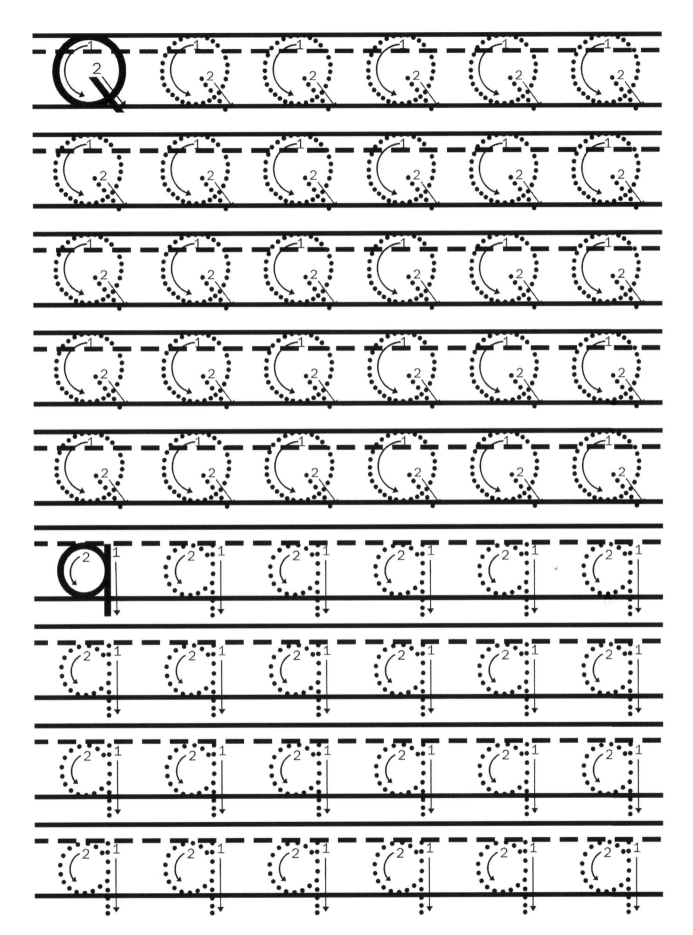

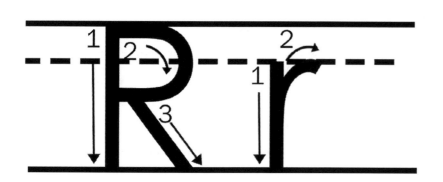

rose

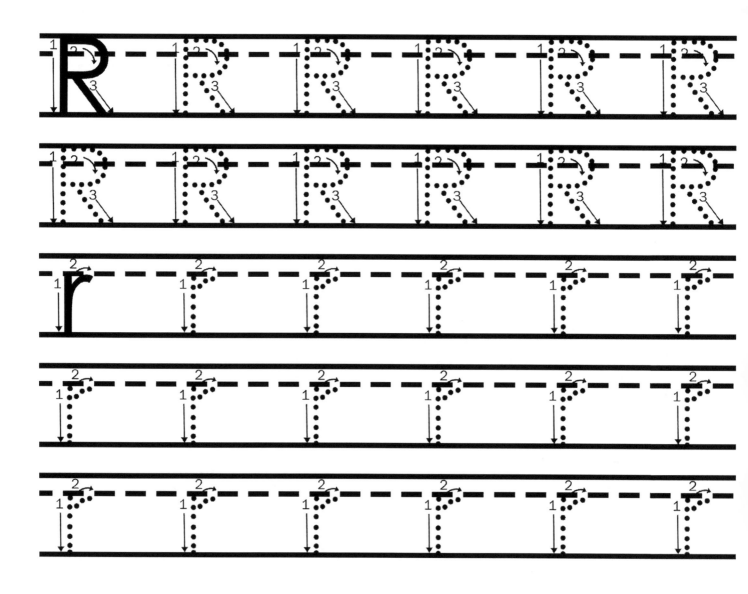

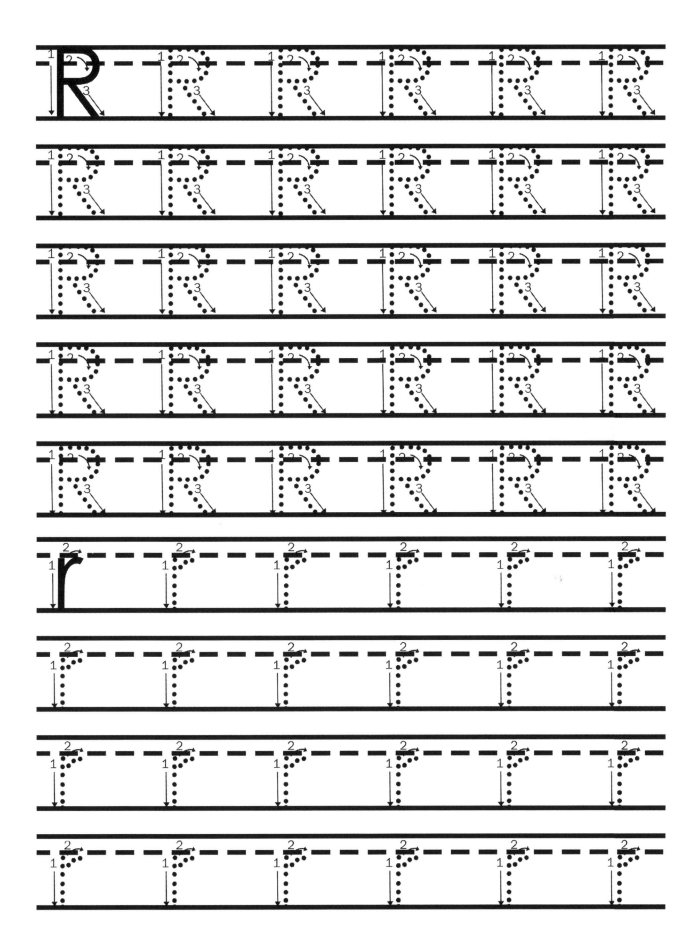

sun

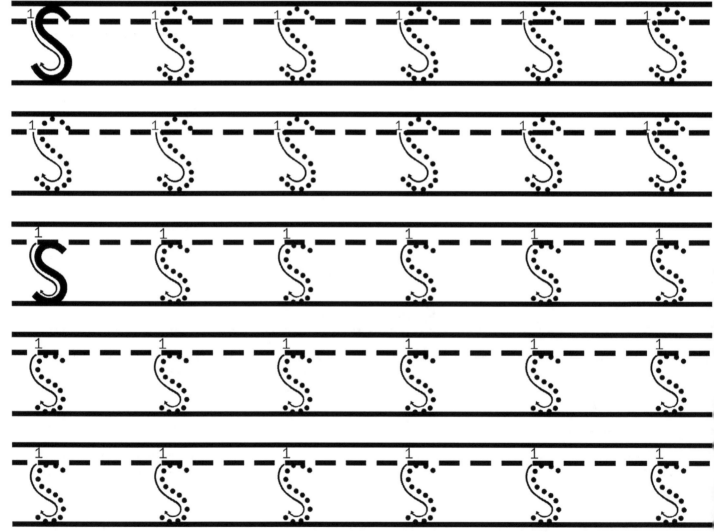

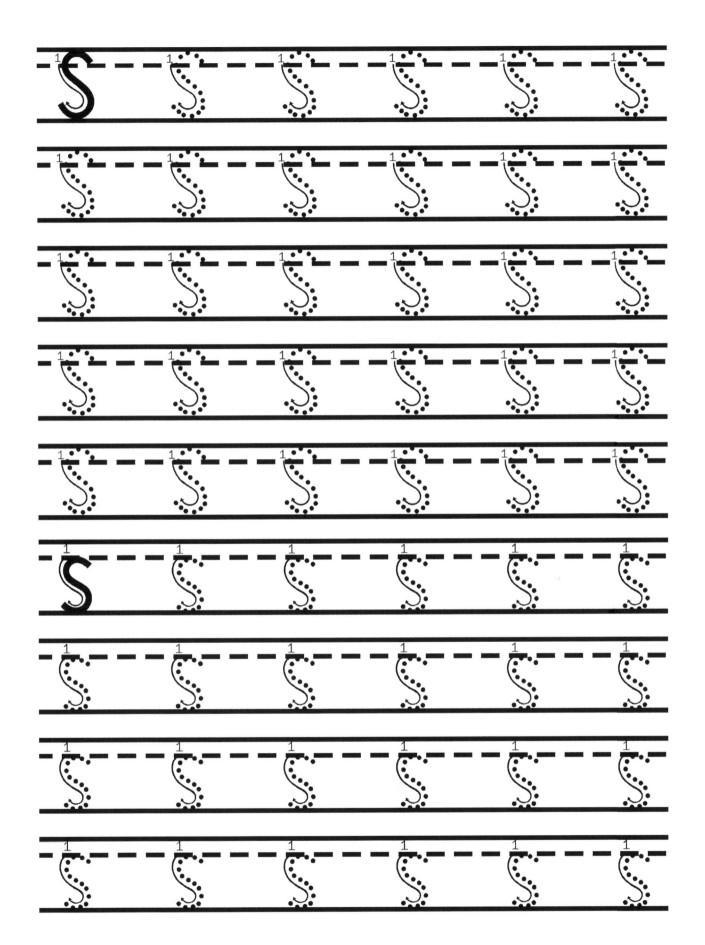

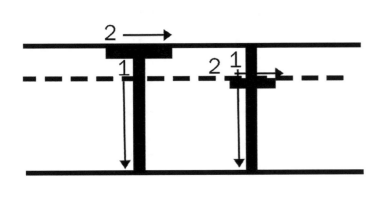

tree

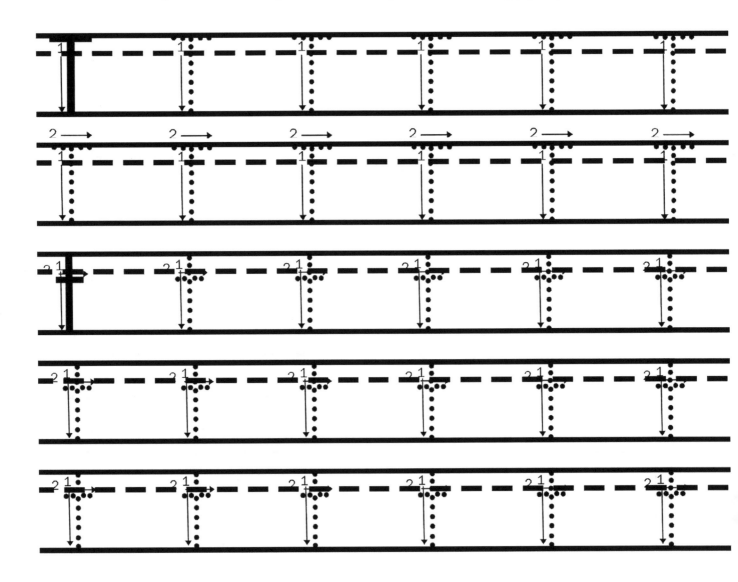

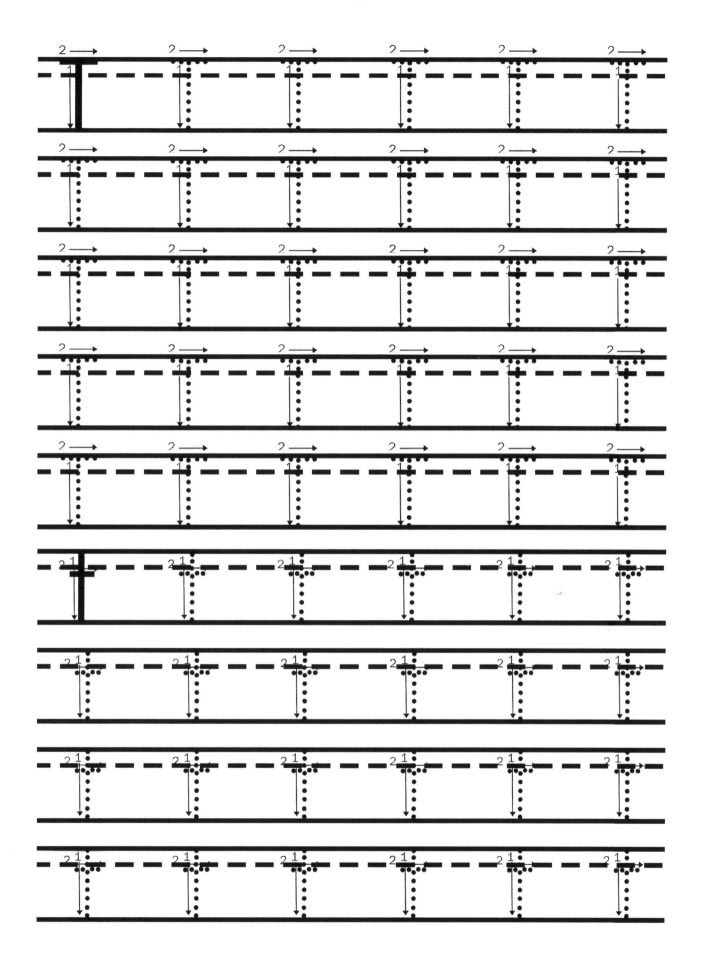

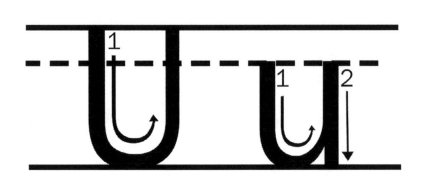

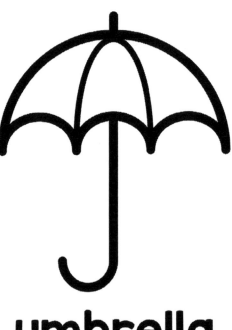

umbrella

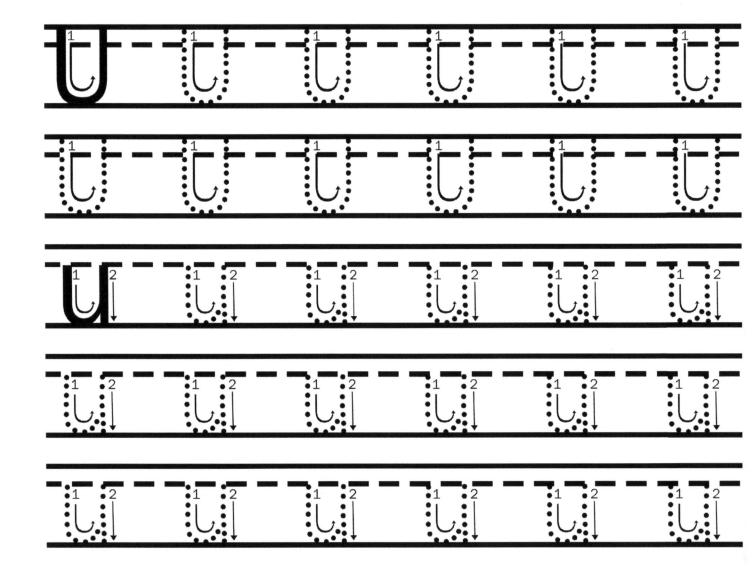

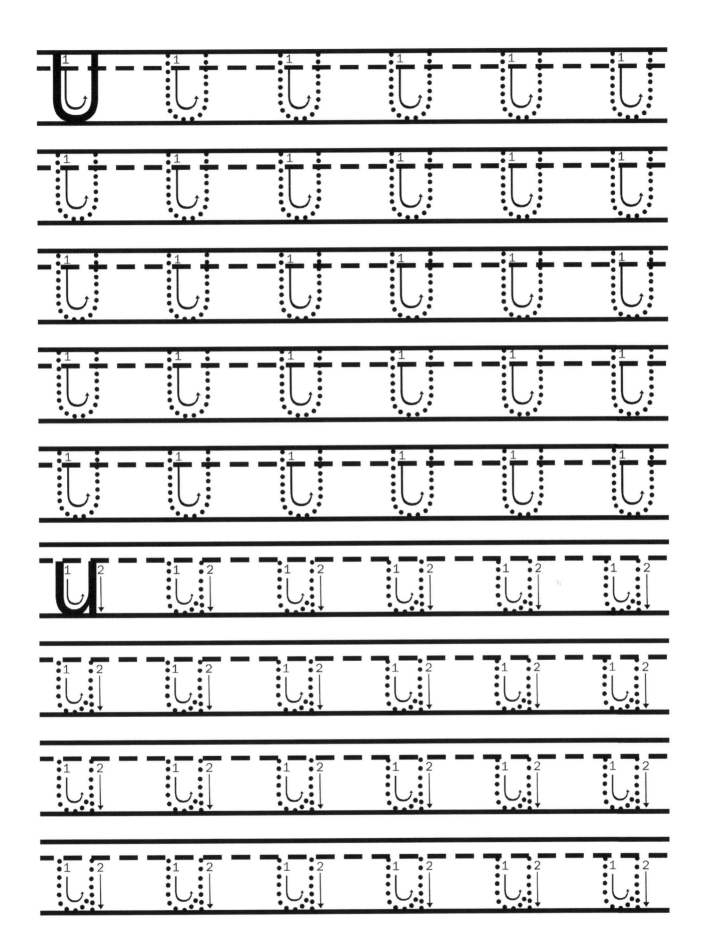

67

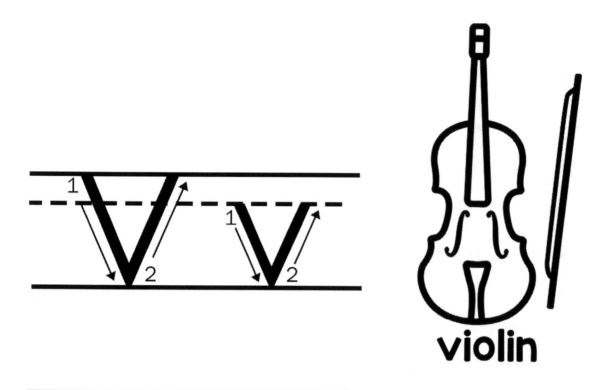

violin

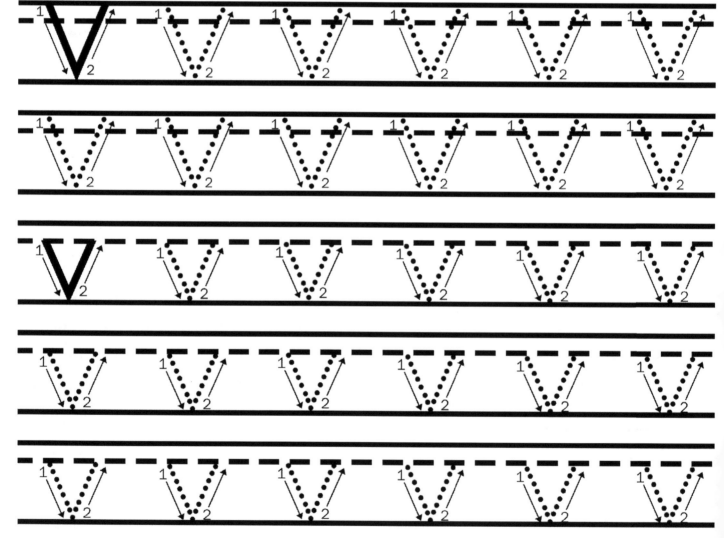

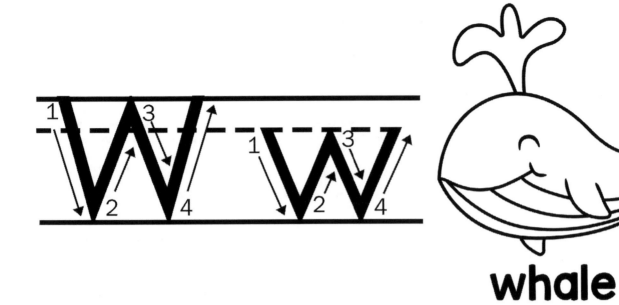

whale

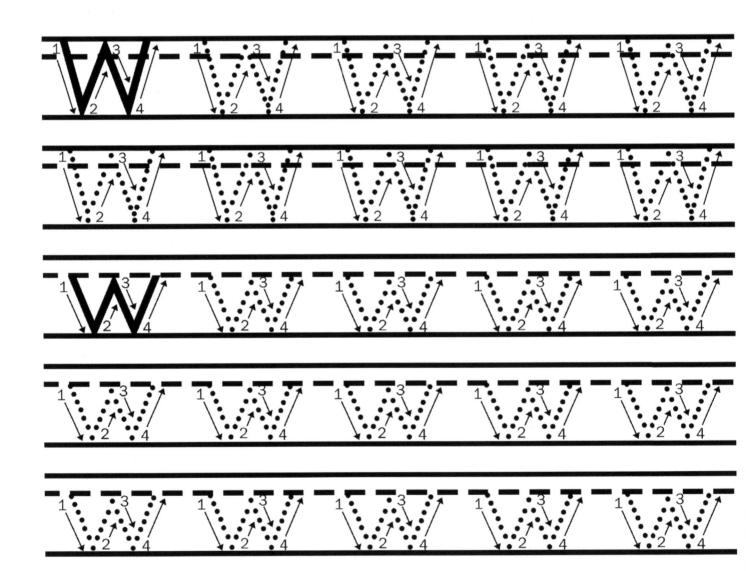

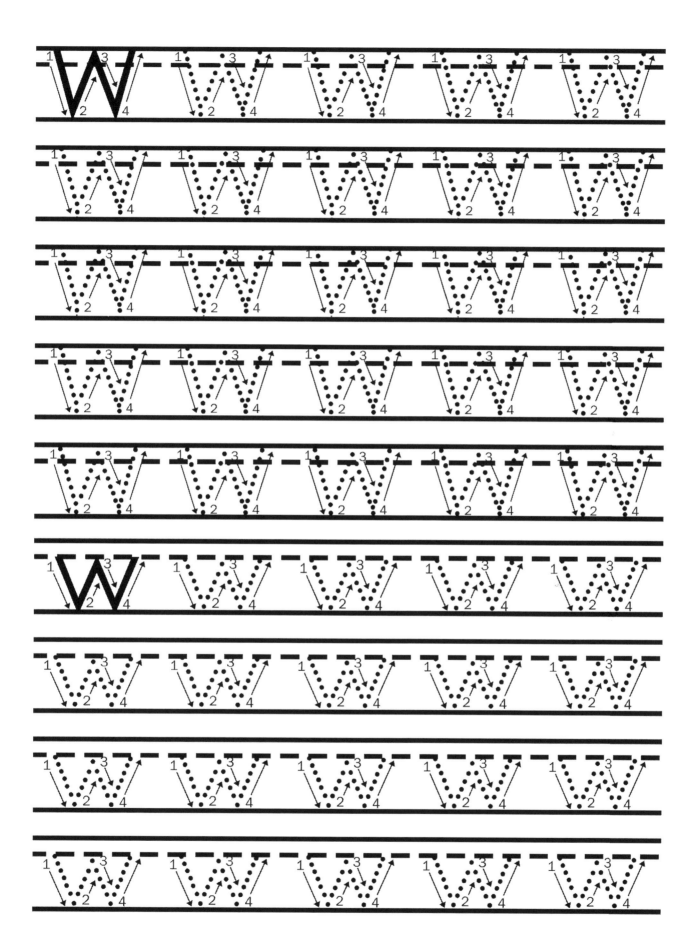

71

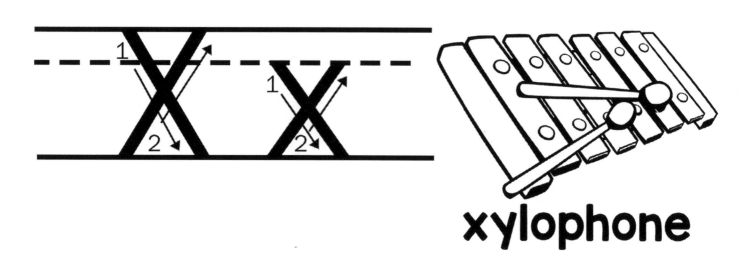

xylophone

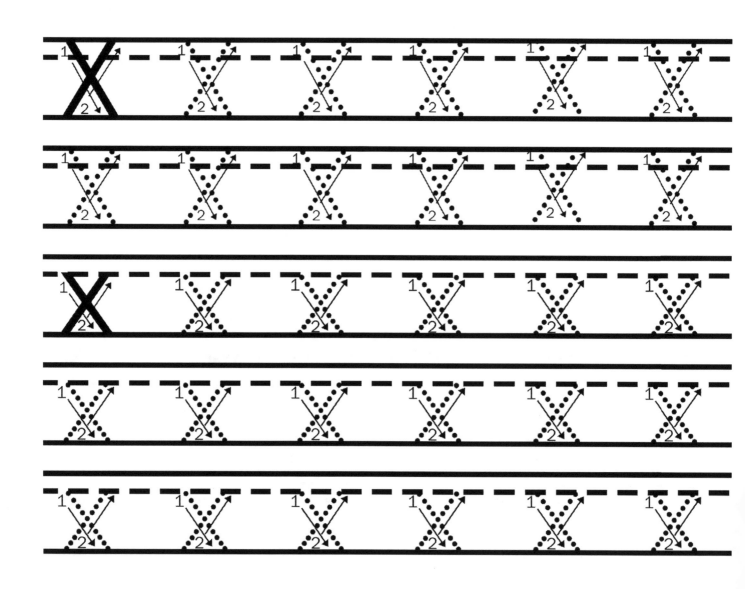

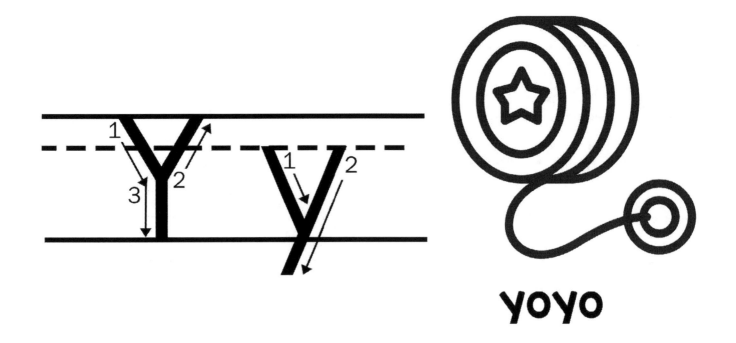

yoyo

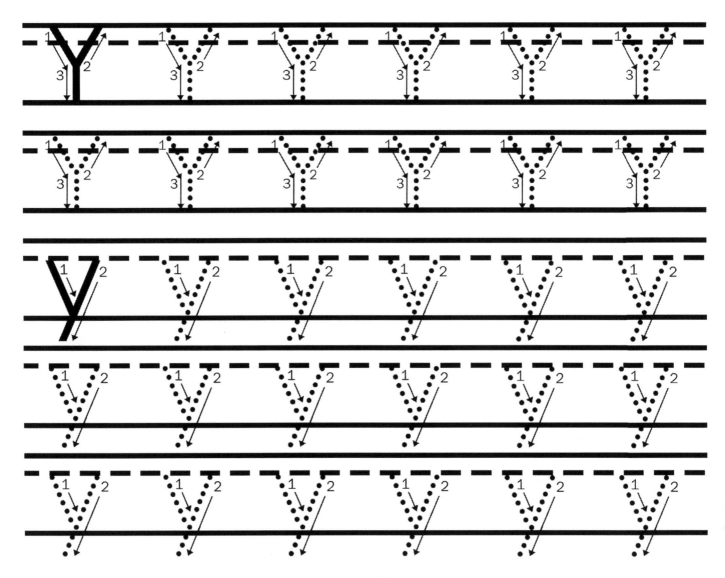

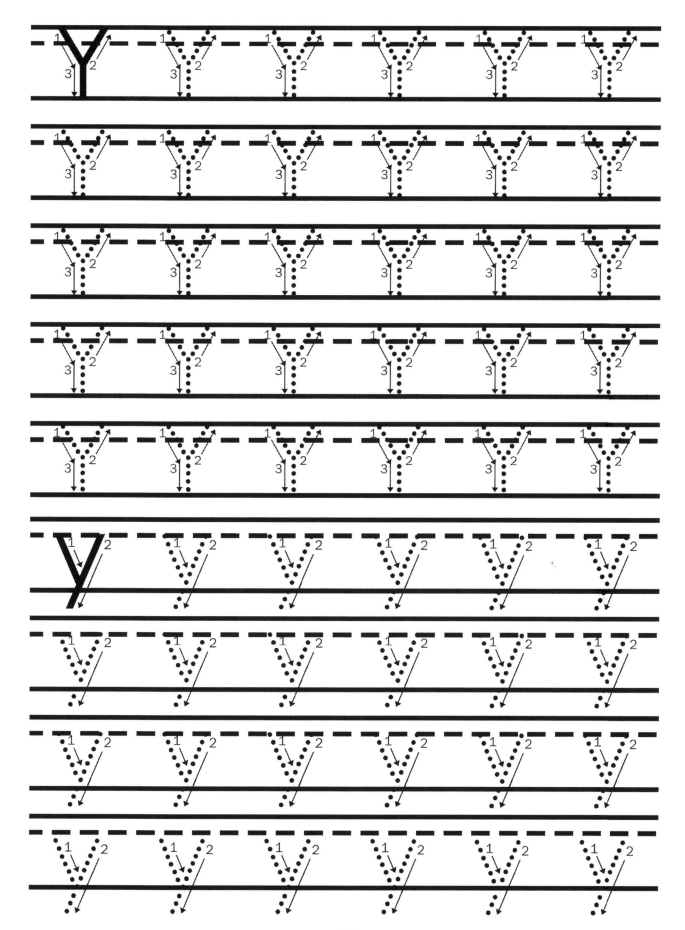

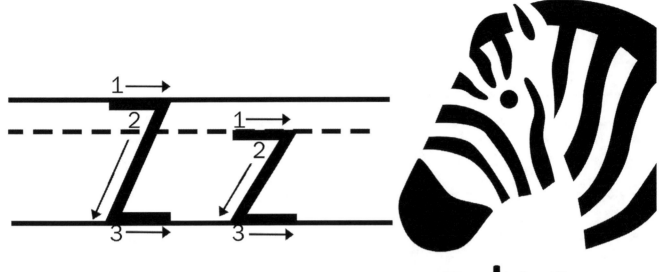

zebra

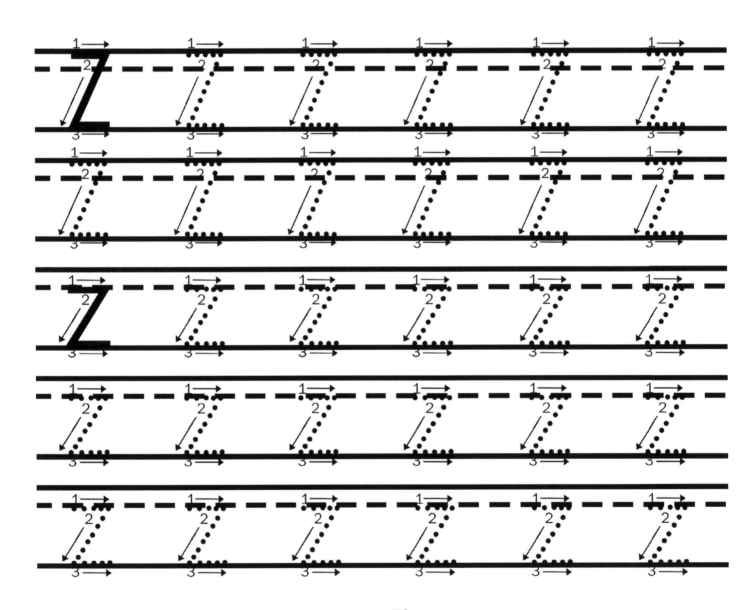

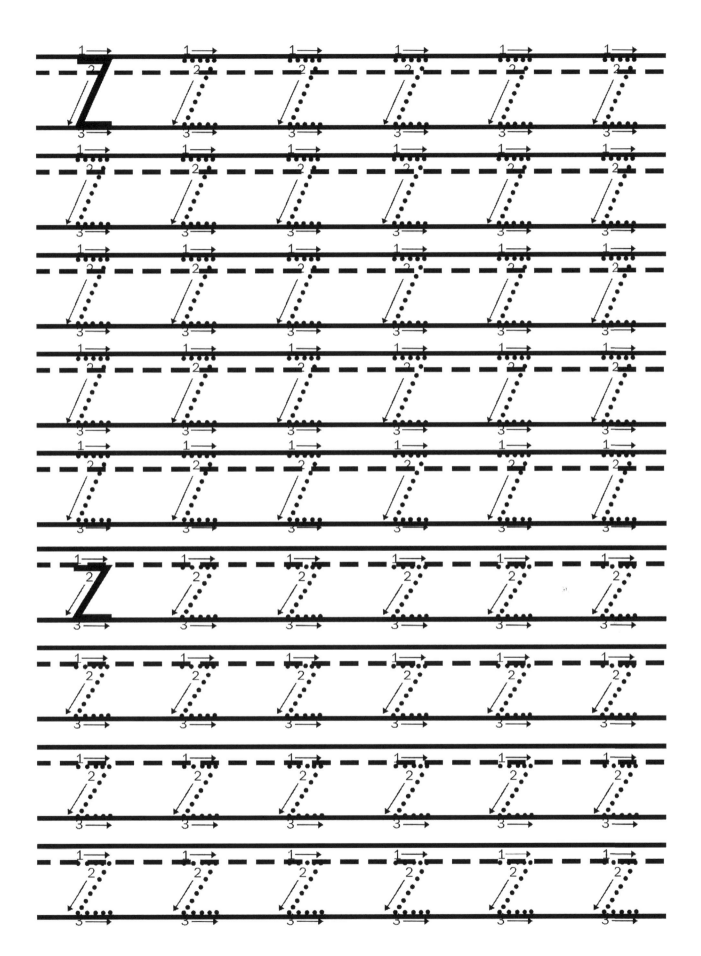

Station 3: Learning to write words and sentences

Very well done.

Now that you have learned the alphabet, we can take it a step further.

In this station we are going to learn how to write words and sentences.
You'll also find a complete overview of the alphabet
and fun writing games.

Let's go!

Trace the lines of the prescribed words!

82

bee   bee

bee   bee

bee   bee

bee   bee

bee   bee

bee   bee

bee   bee

cat　　　　cat

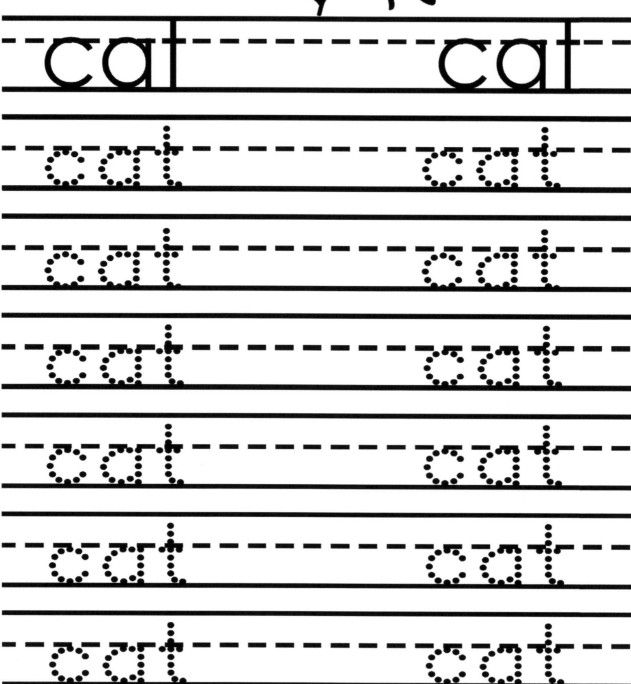

cat　　　cat

cat　　　cat

cat　　　cat

cat　　　cat

cat　　　cat

cat　　　cat

dog   dog

dog   dog

dog   dog

dog   dog

dog   dog

dog   dog

dog   dog

elephant

elephant

elephant

elephant

elephant

elephant

elephant

flower flower

flower flower

flower flower

flower flower

flower flower

flower flower

flower flower

giraffe giraffe

giraffe giraffe

giraffe giraffe

giraffe giraffe

giraffe giraffe

giraffe giraffe

giraffe giraffe

house house

house house

house house

house house

house house

house house

house house

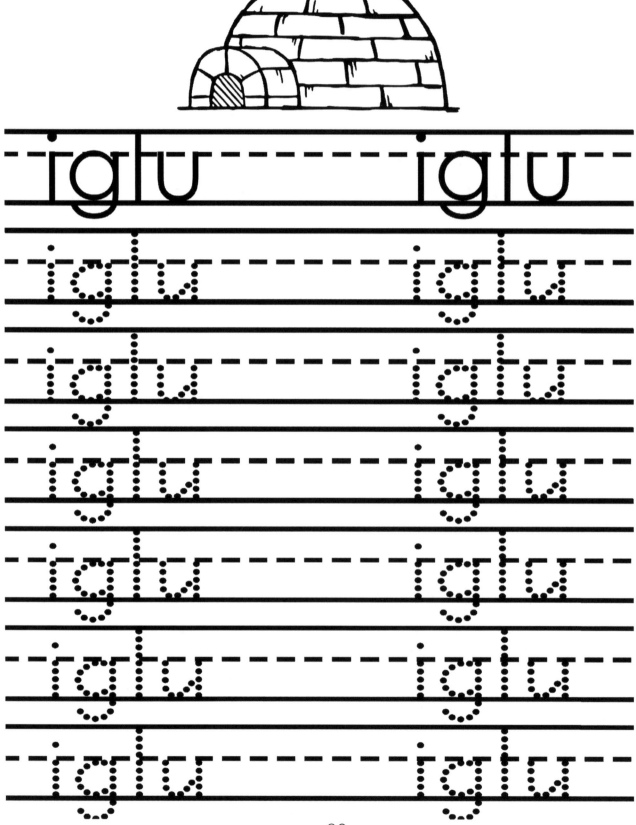

iglu   iglu

iglu   iglu

iglu   iglu

iglu   iglu

iglu   iglu

iglu   iglu

iglu   iglu

jellyfish

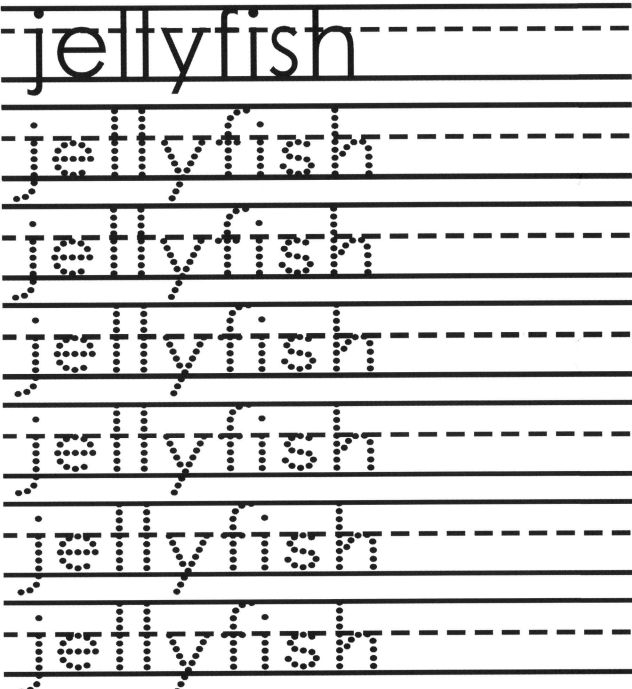

jellyfish

jellyfish

jellyfish

jellyfish

jellyfish

jellyfish

king king

king king

king king

king king

king king

king king

king king

lion   lion

lion   lion

lion   lion

lion   lion

lion   lion

lion   lion

lion   lion

moon ‑ ‑ moon

moon ‑ ‑ moon

moon ‑ ‑ moon

moon ‑ ‑ moon

moon ‑ ‑ moon

moon ‑ ‑ moon

moon ‑ ‑ moon

nest   nest

nest   nest

nest   nest

nest   nest

nest   nest

nest   nest

nest   nest

ow | ow | ow

ow | ow | ow

ow | ow | ow

ow | ow | ow

ow | ow | ow

ow | ow | ow

ow | ow | ow

panda   panda

panda   panda

panda   panda

panda   panda

panda   panda

panda   panda

panda   panda

queen   queen

queen   queen

queen   queen

queen   queen

queen   queen

queen   queen

queen   queen

rose   rose

rose   rose

rose   rose

rose   rose

rose   rose

rose   rose

rose   rose

sun sun sun

sun sun sun

sun sun sun

sun sun sun

sun sun sun

sun sun sun

sun sun sun

tree   tree

tree   tree

tree   tree

tree   tree

tree   tree

tree   tree

tree   tree

umbretta

umbrella

umbrella

umbrella

umbrella

umbrella

umbrella

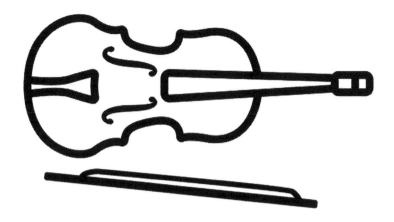

violin violin

violin violin

violin violin

violin violin

violin violin

violin violin

violin violin

whale   whale

whale   whale

whale   whale

whale   whale

whale   whale

whale   whale

whale   whale

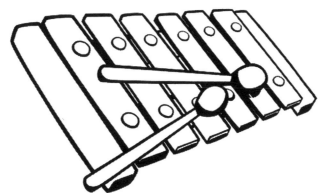

xylophone

xylophone

xylophone

xylophone

xylophone

xylophone

xylophone

yoyo yoyo

yoyo yoyo

yoyo yoyo

yoyo yoyo

yoyo yoyo

yoyo yoyo

yoyo yoyo

zebra   zebra

zebra   zebra

zebra   zebra

zebra   zebra

zebra   zebra

zebra   zebra

zebra   zebra

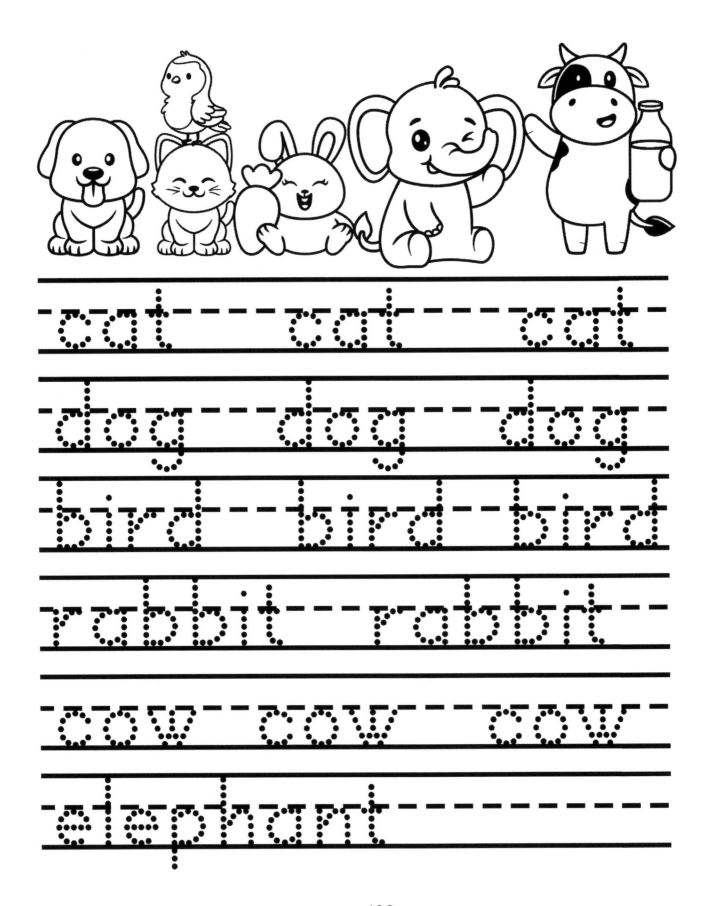

cat   cat   cat

dog   dog   dog

bird   bird   bird

rabbit   rabbit

cow   cow   cow

elephant

pants   pants

dress   dress

skirt   skirt

blouse   blouse

shoes   shoes

mom mom mom

dad dad dad

brother brother

sister sister

grandmother

grandfather

pizza pizza pizza

ice cream

cake cake cake

eggs eggs eggs

hamburger

lawyer

policeman

actress

teacher

painter

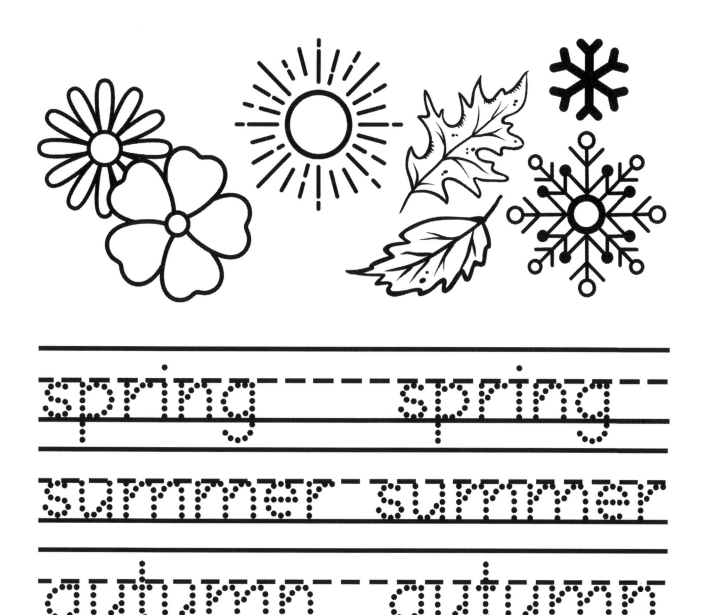

spring   spring

summer summer

autumn autumn

winter winter

I love summer.

I like to swim.

Today is a beautiful day

I like to read.

Life is beautiful.

I am looking forward
to school.

I love my parents

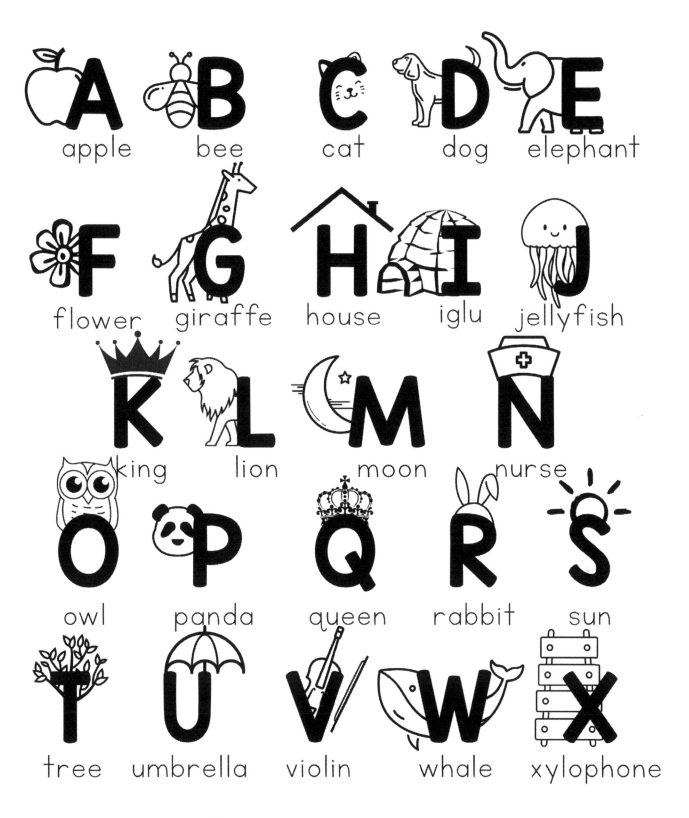

apple bee cat dog elephant

flower giraffe house iglu jellyfish

king lion moon nurse

owl panda queen rabbit sun

tree umbrella violin whale xylophone

yoyo zebra

Station 4: Learning numbers

Now it's time for something new!

You've come this far:
Now you're ready to get to know the numbers.

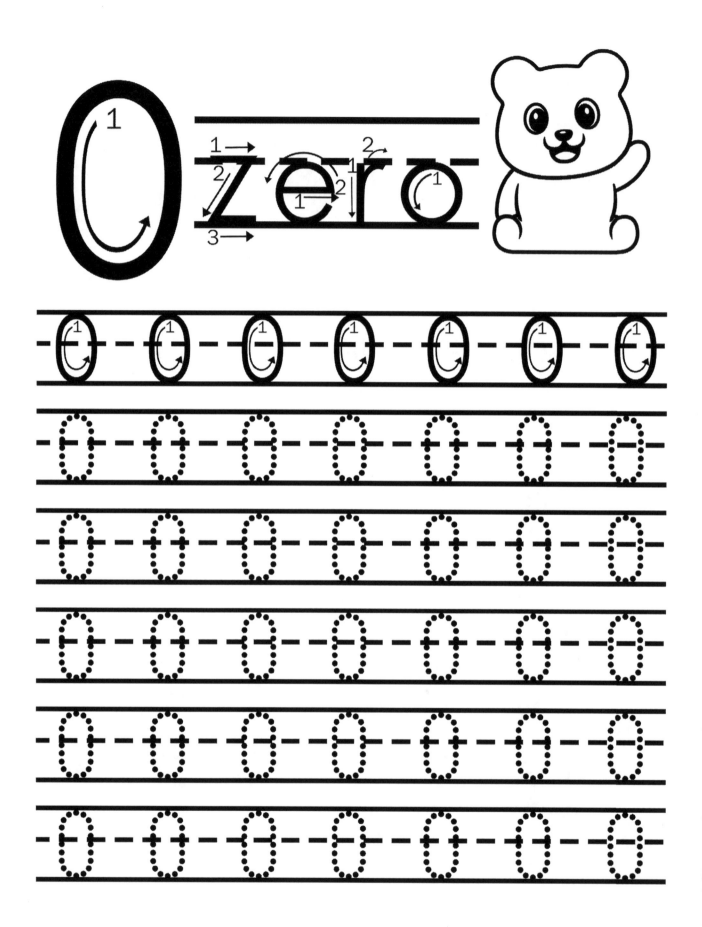

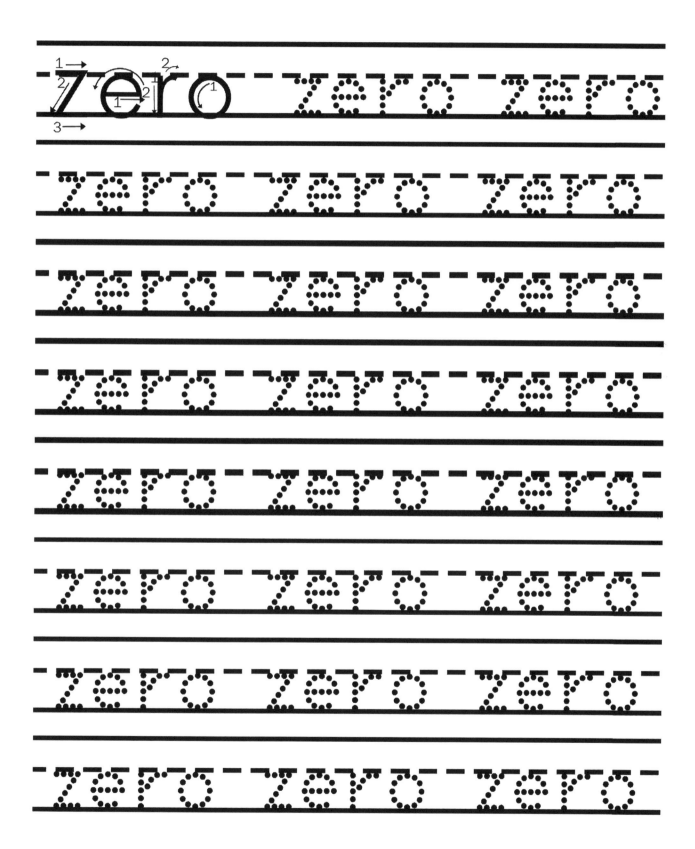

125

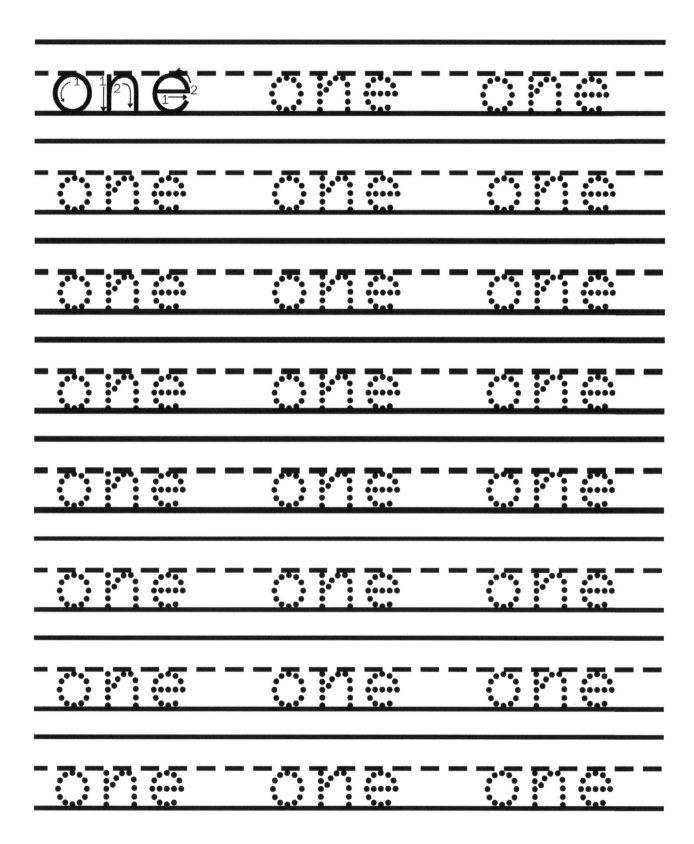

127

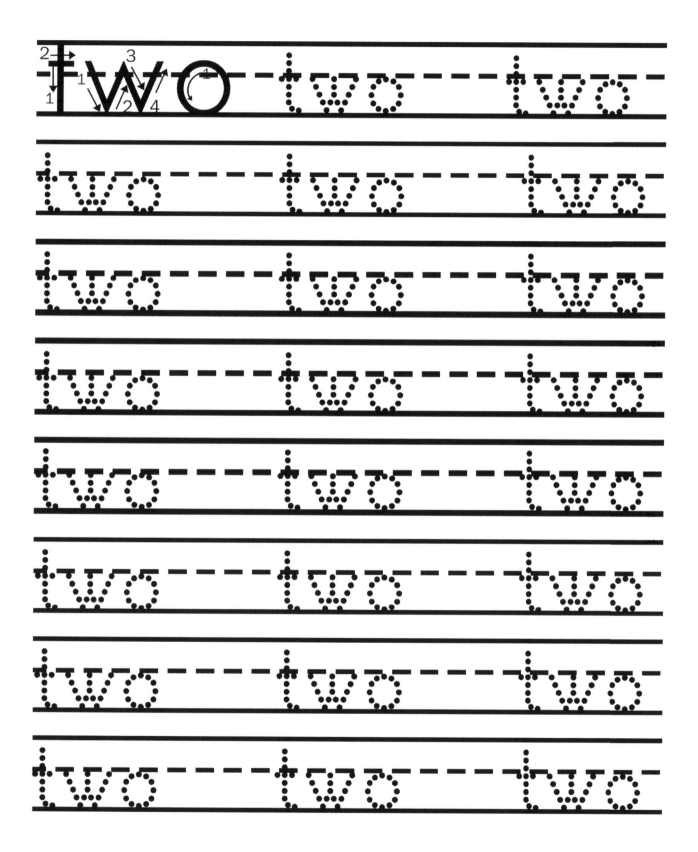

129

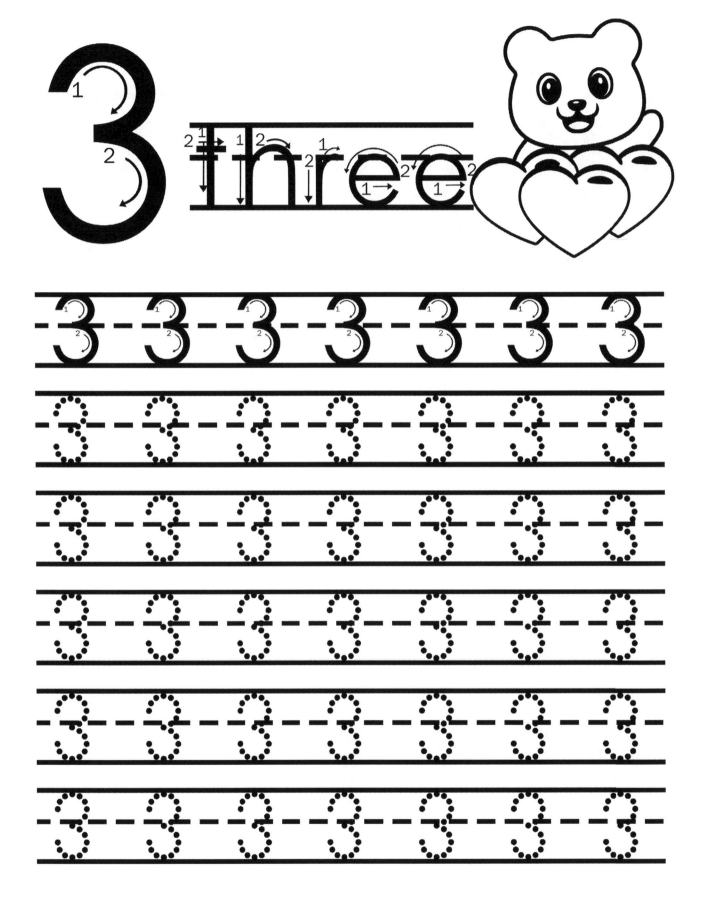

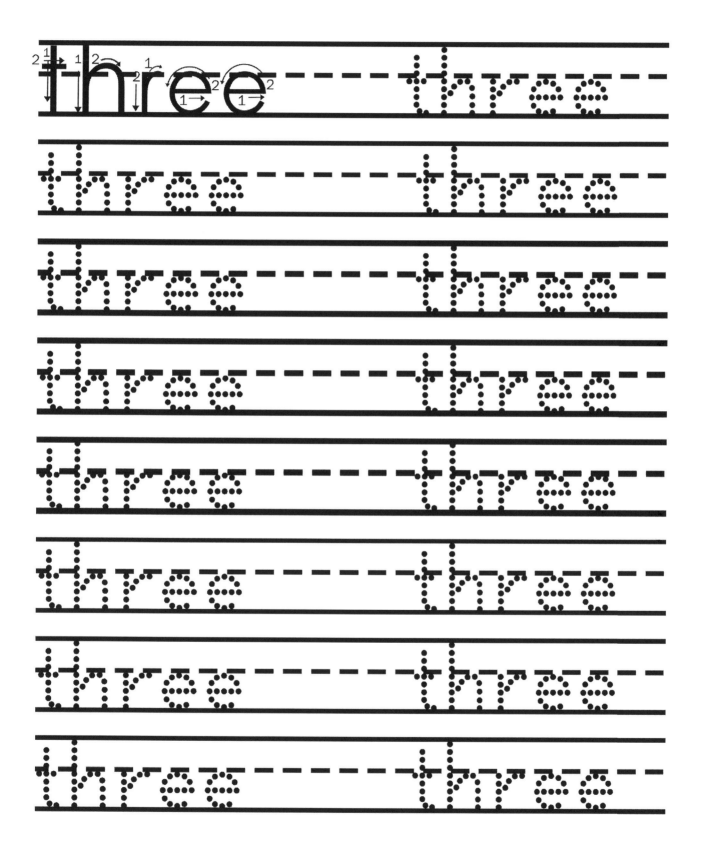

four

four four four

four four four

four four four

four four four

four four four

four four four

four four four

four four four

five

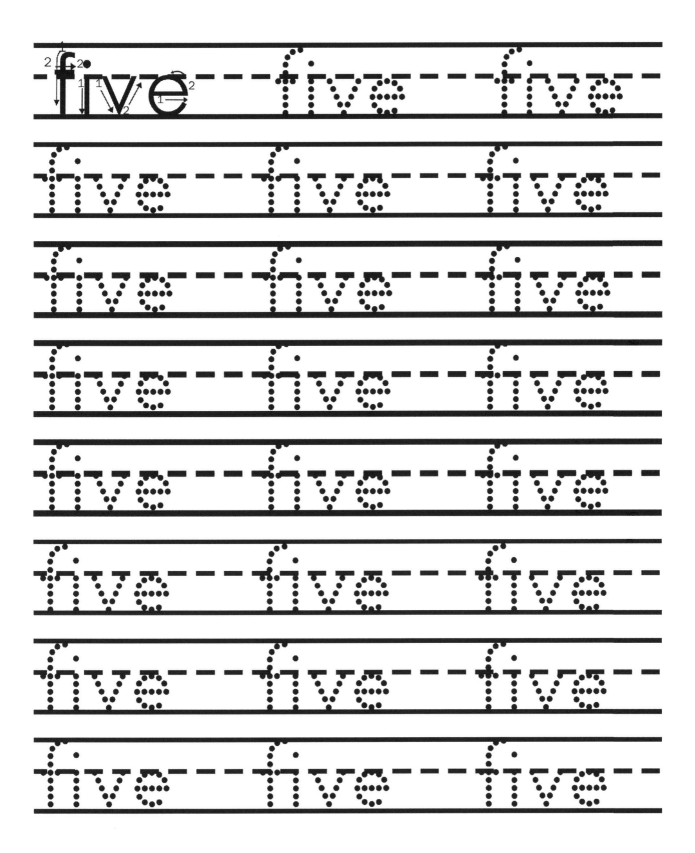

135

six

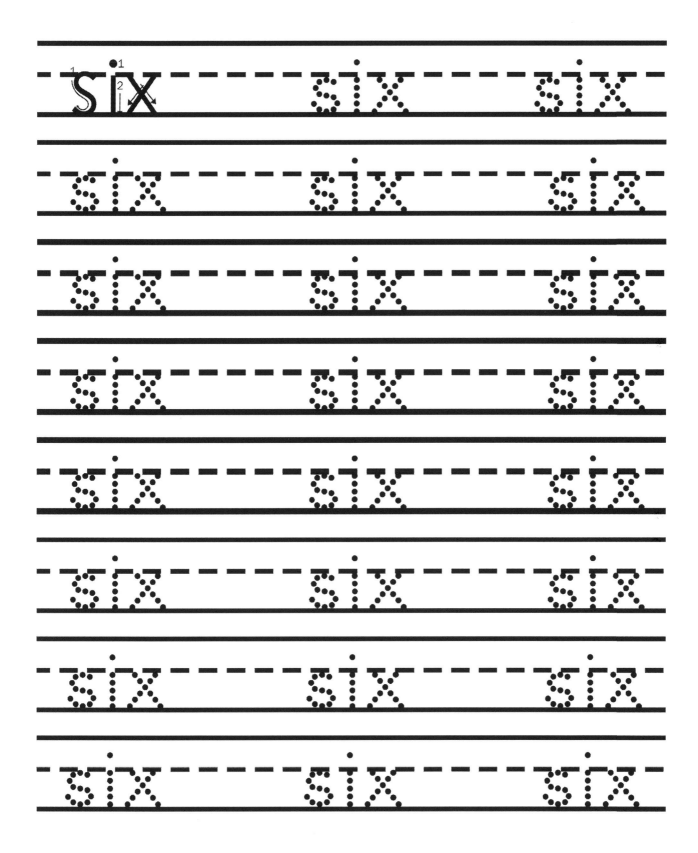

137

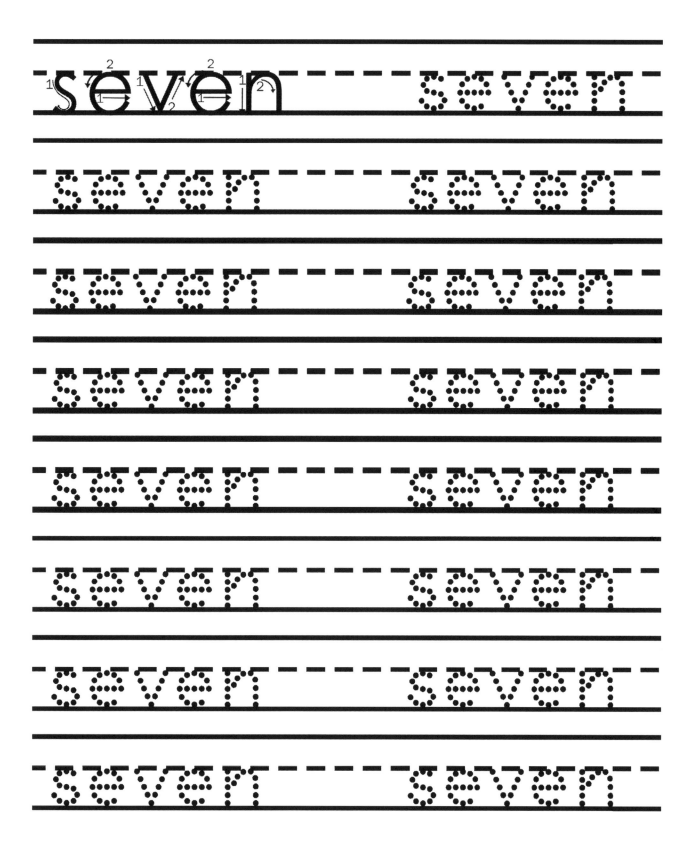

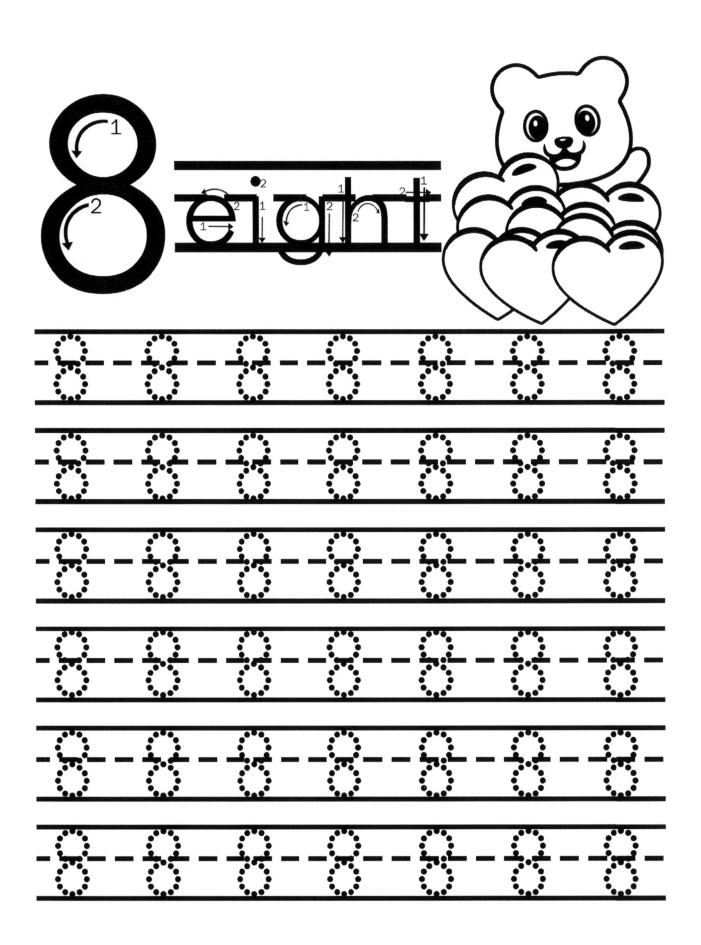

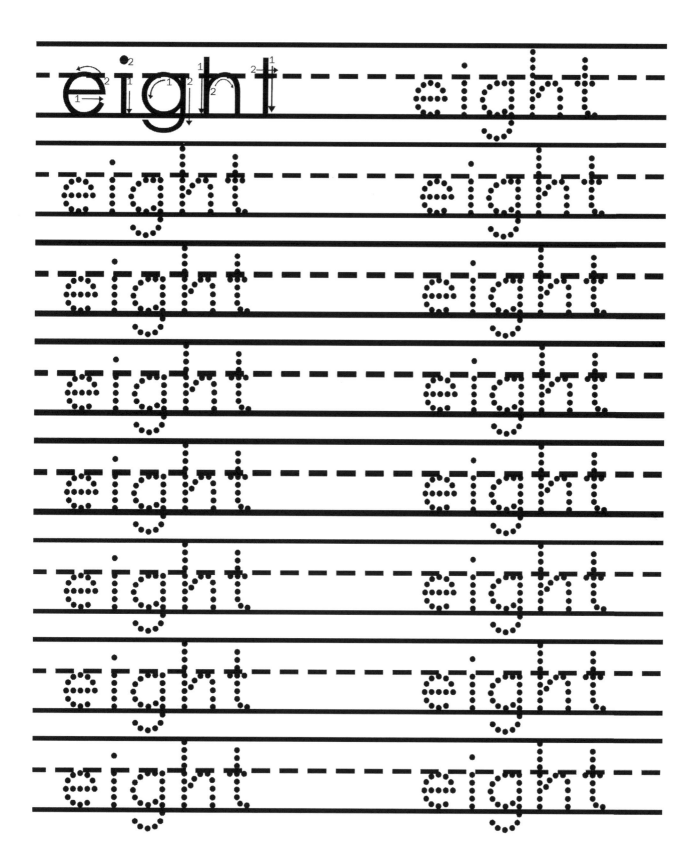

141

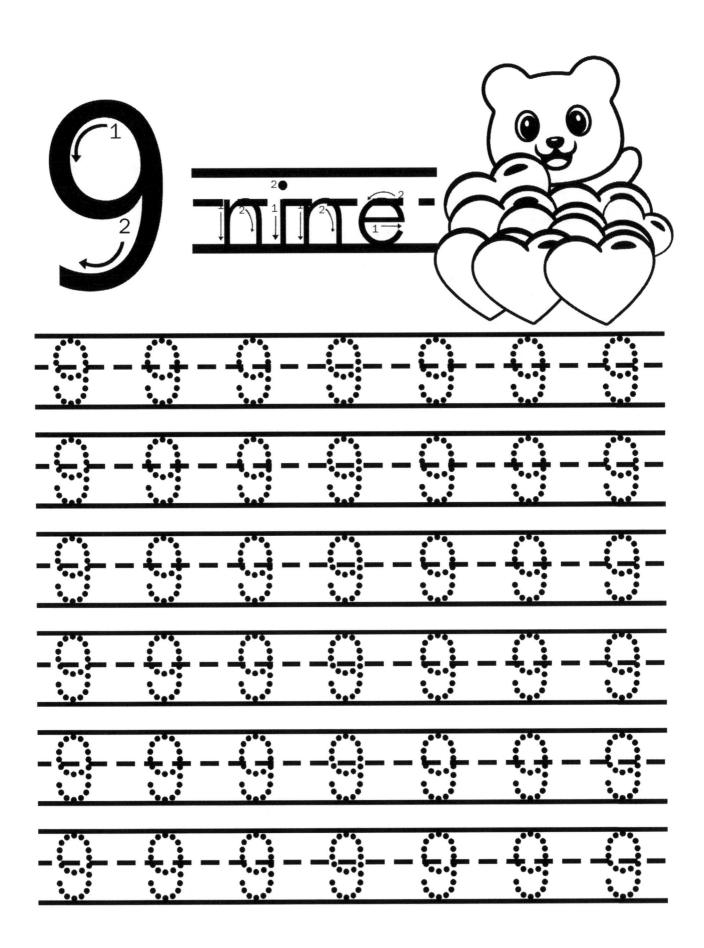

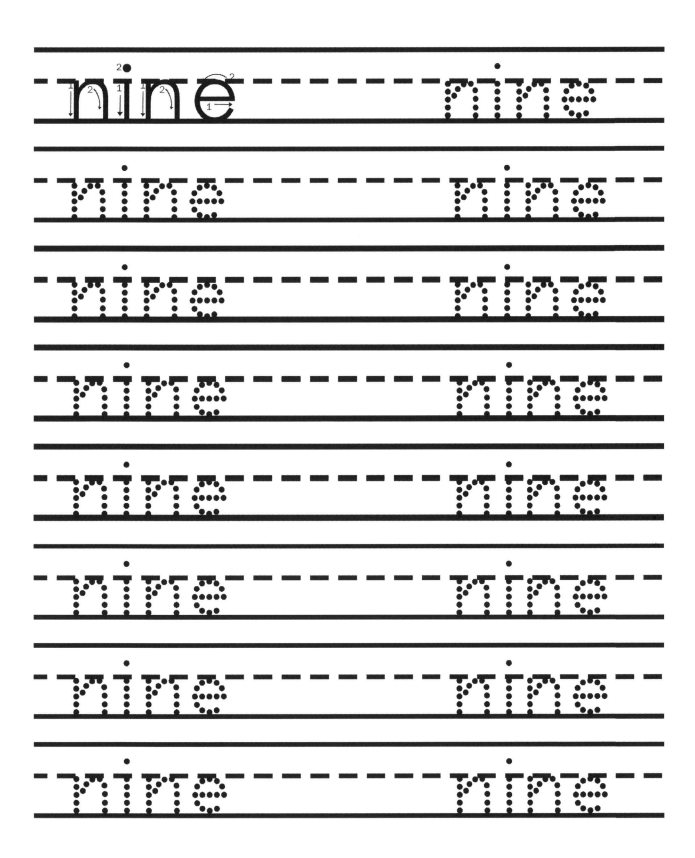

143

1 1 1 1 1 1 1

2 2 2 2 2 2 2

3 3 3 3 3 3 3

4 4 4 4 4 4 4

5 5 5 5 5 5 5

6 6 6 6 6 6 6

7 7 7 7 7 7 7

8 8 8 8 8 8 8

9 9 9 9 9 9 9

10 10 10 10 10

Station 5: Learning mathematics

Welcome to a new station.

Here you'll find fun math exercises
and test your new knowledge.

	1 1 1 1 1
	2 2 2 2 2
	3 3 3 3 3
	4 4 4 4 4
	5 5 5 5 5
	6 6 6 6 6
	7 7 7 7 7
	8 8 8 8 8
	9 9 9 9 9
	10 10 10 10 10

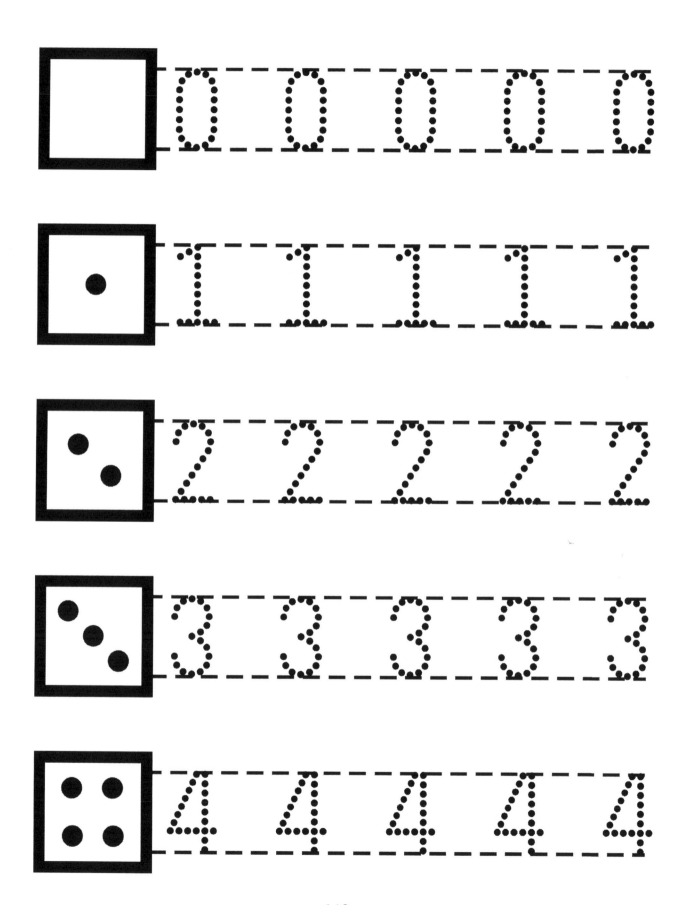

0 0 0 0 0

1 1 1 1 1

2 2 2 2 2

3 3 3 3 3

4 4 4 4 4

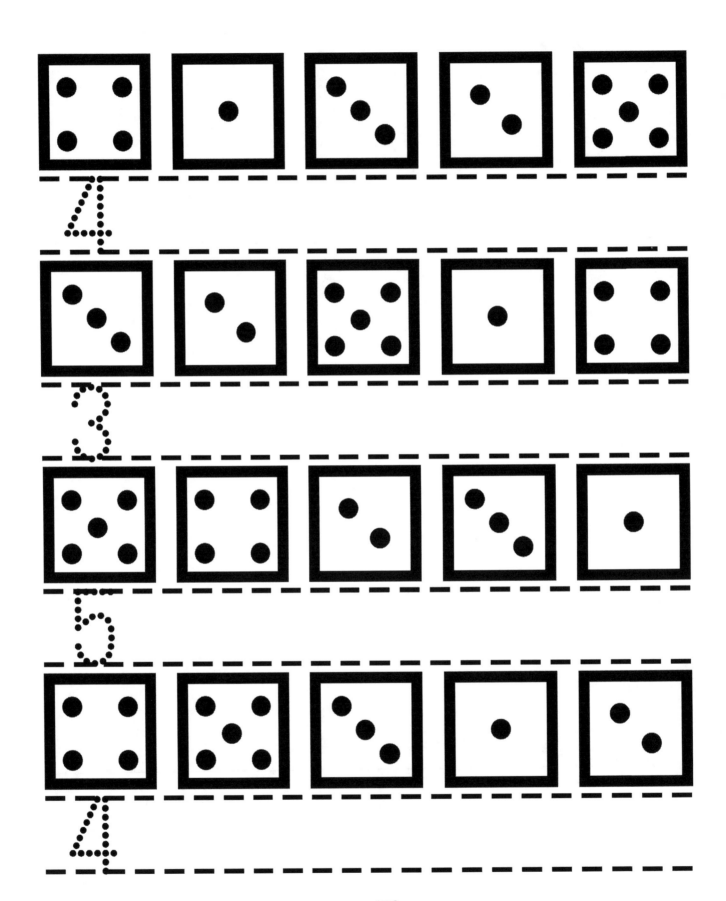

150

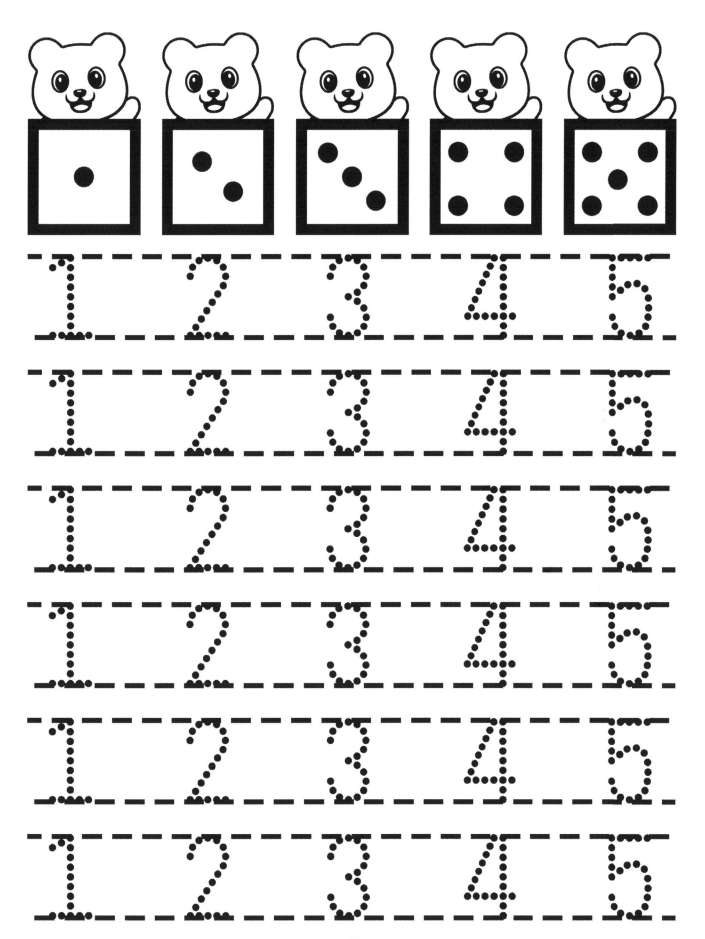

Draw the right shape around the dots

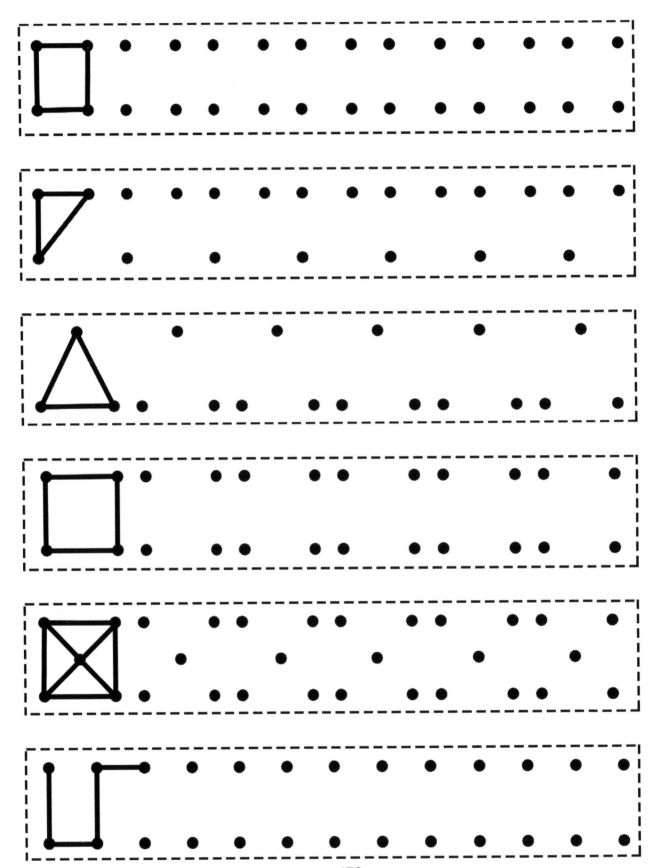

Draw the right shape around the numbers

How many can you count? Circle correctly.

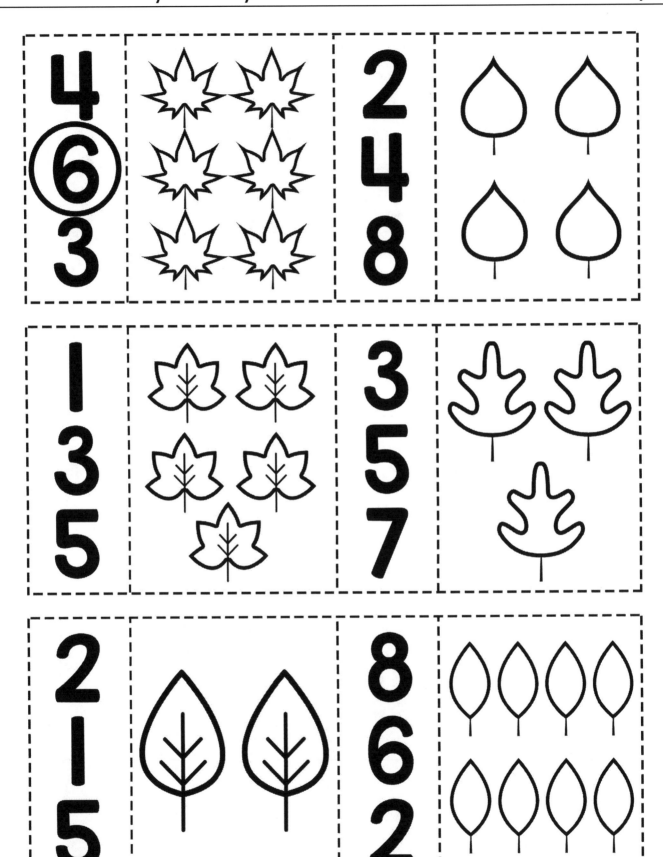

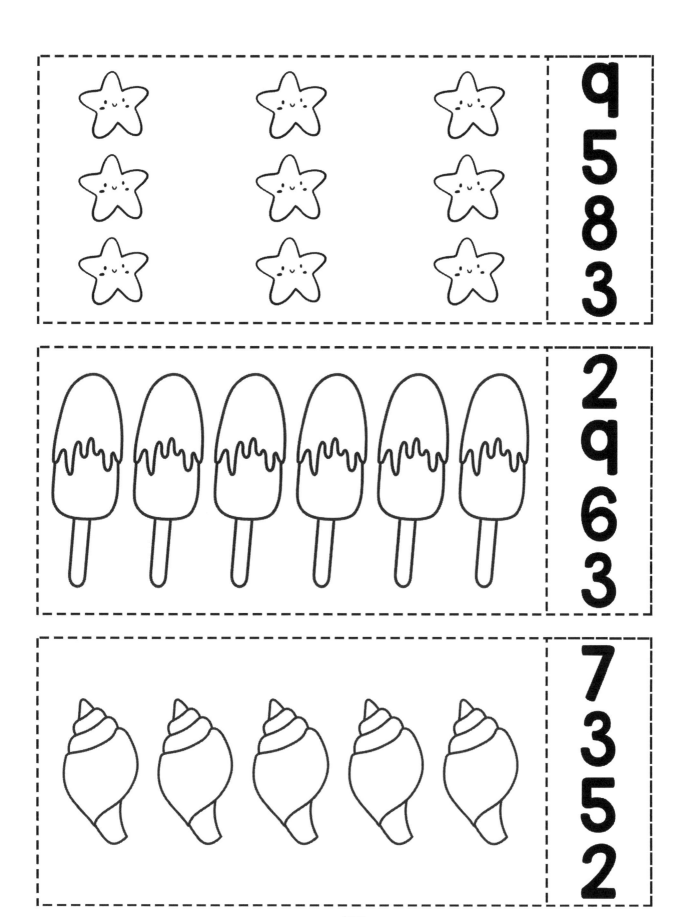

4
2
5
3

3
7
8
2

2
5
6
8

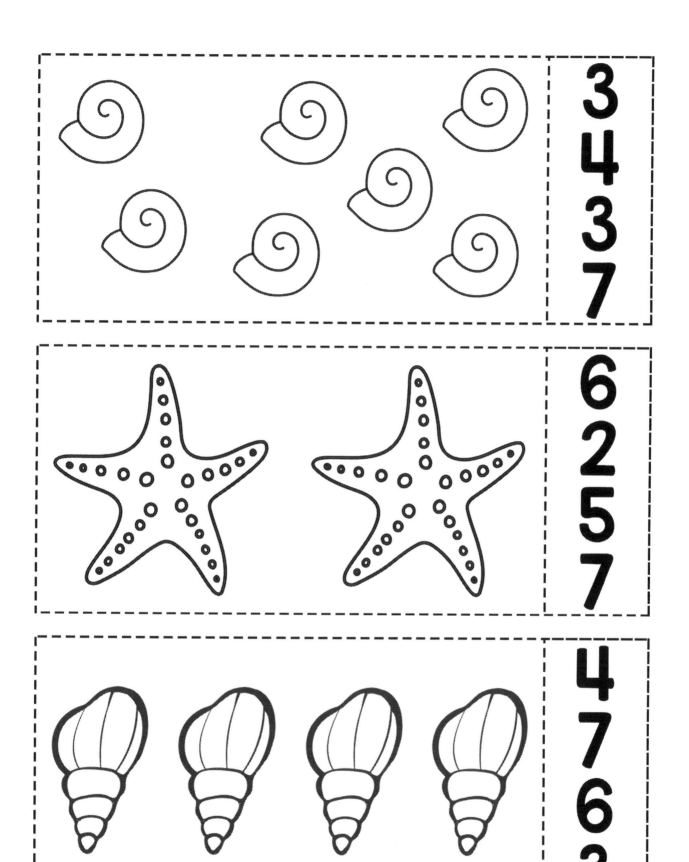

2
5
3
8

7
4
5
8

5
3
6
2

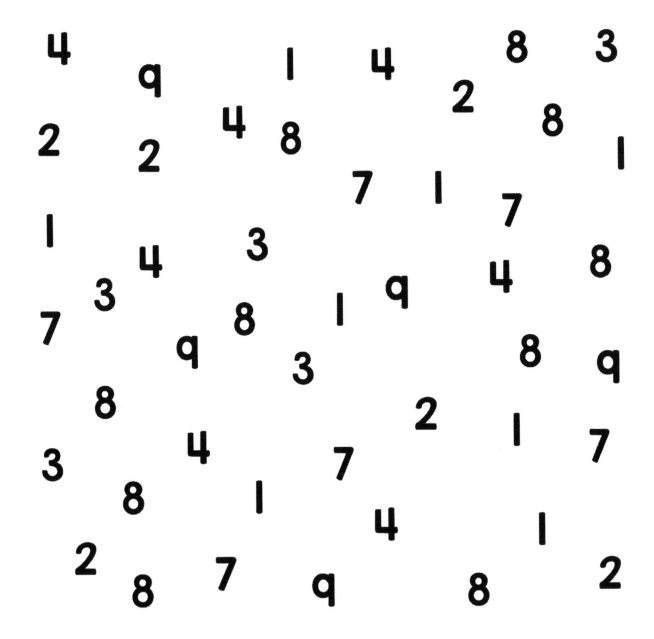

7 q 1 7 2 ц
2 2 7 ц 8 ц
8 q 3 q 2 8 8
1 8 q ц
3 8 1 2 1 ц
1 3 3
3 2 8 1 ц 7 3
1 8 1 8 8 q
1 7 8 7 8

8 1 q   7   2 4
3   4 7   q   2   8   4
    2   q   1   7   8   1   7
1   4   8   2   1   3   4
          q   3   8   7   1
   4   3   2   2
7   3   3
   q   1 1   7 8   8
8 8   1 8   1   7
      7

2   5   1   7   8   2   4

5   4   8

7   8   8   q   2   5   4

q   1   8

5   1   7   q   7   1   7

3   8   2   5   3   4

q   1   7   1   5

4   q   3   2   8   q

3   1

7   1   8   1   3   4 7

8   1   5   2

5

5   7   1   4

Who is looking to the left and who is looking to the right?
Write the number in the box.

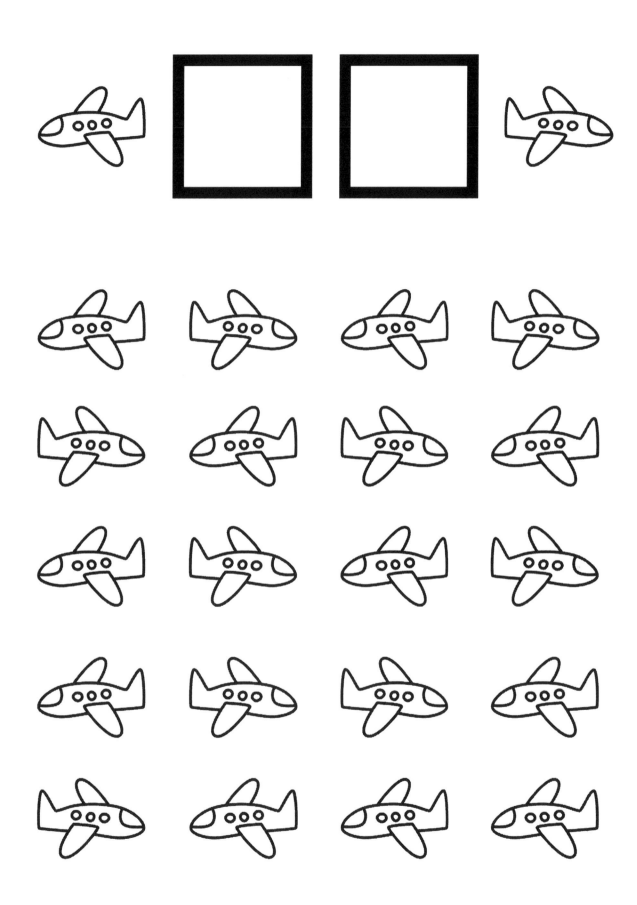

Station 6: Learning how to paint

Phuu now we have calculated and written enough.

Let's relex a little and do something different - how about painting? I can't wait.

Let's get the colors and get started.

Paint me!

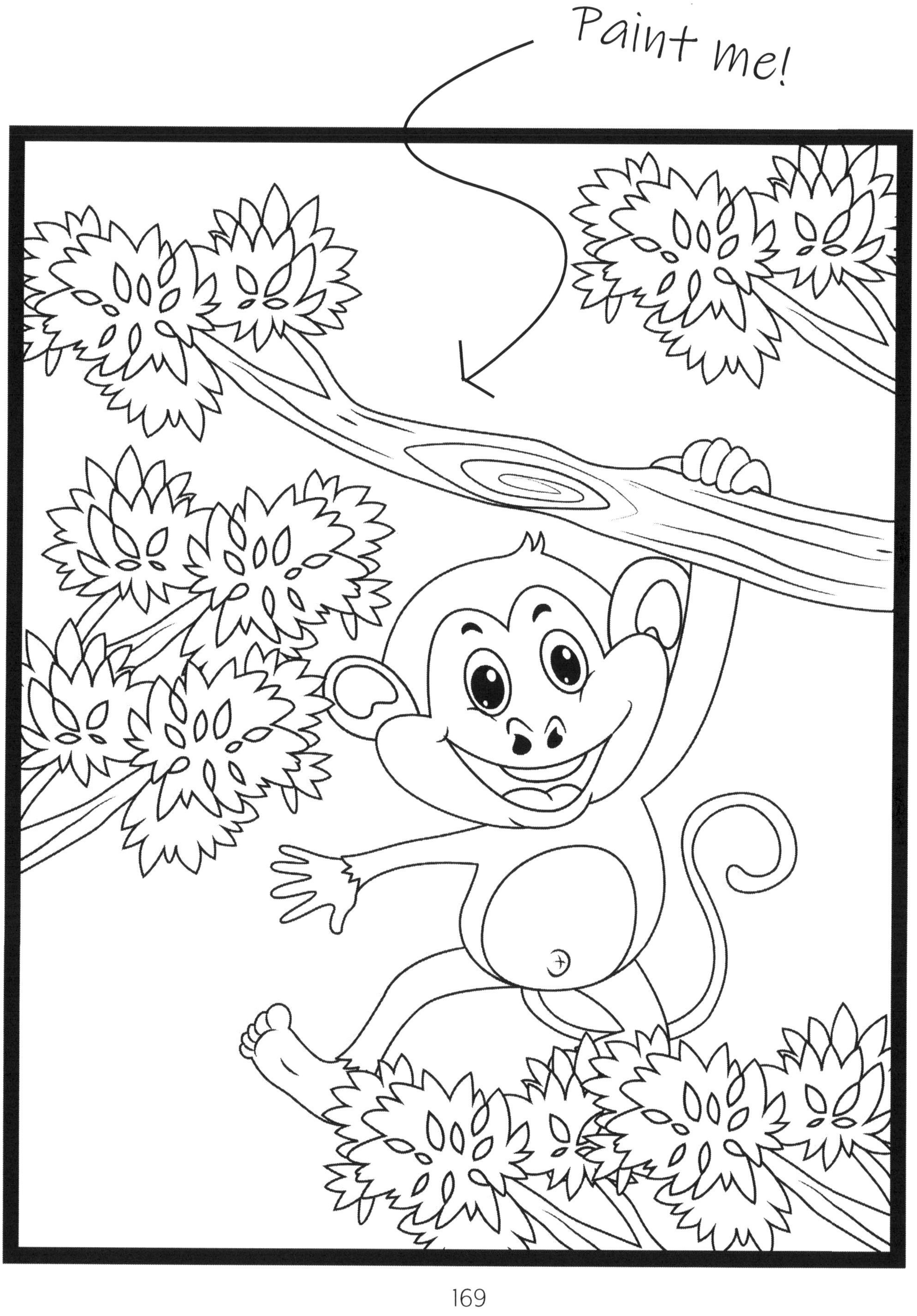
Paint me!

Paint the leaves in the right color

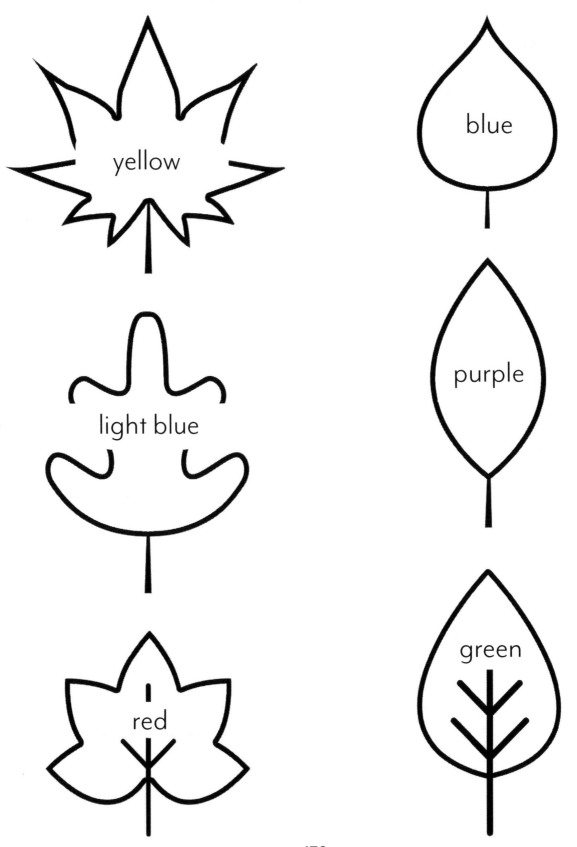

yellow

blue

light blue

purple

red

green

Paint by numbers.
Paint correctly!

1 = brown

2 = green

3 = red

4 = dark brown

5 = yellow

1 = pink

2 = green

3 = yellow

4= red

1 = white

2 = yelllow

3 = pink

4 = brown

5 = black

1 = green

2 = yellow

3 yellow and green

1 = brown

2 = dark brown

3 = orange

4= yellow

1 = purple

2 = brown

3 = green

Station 7: Learning how to draw

We have learned something new again
and that means
taking another step forward.
Now that we have painted diligently,
we can try drawing.

There's a little artist in all of us and now it's
time to let it out.

Draw the lines correctly.
Are you wondering what it will be?

Dot to dot!

Connect the numbers in the right order and admire the objects that come up.

186

How are the kids feeling today?
Paint emotions on their faces.

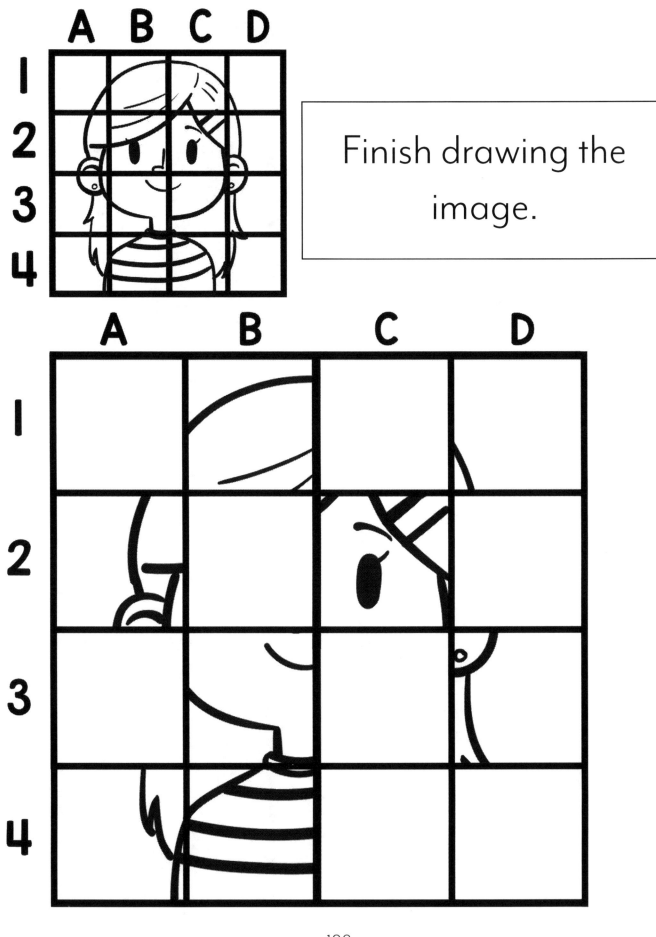

Finish drawing the image.

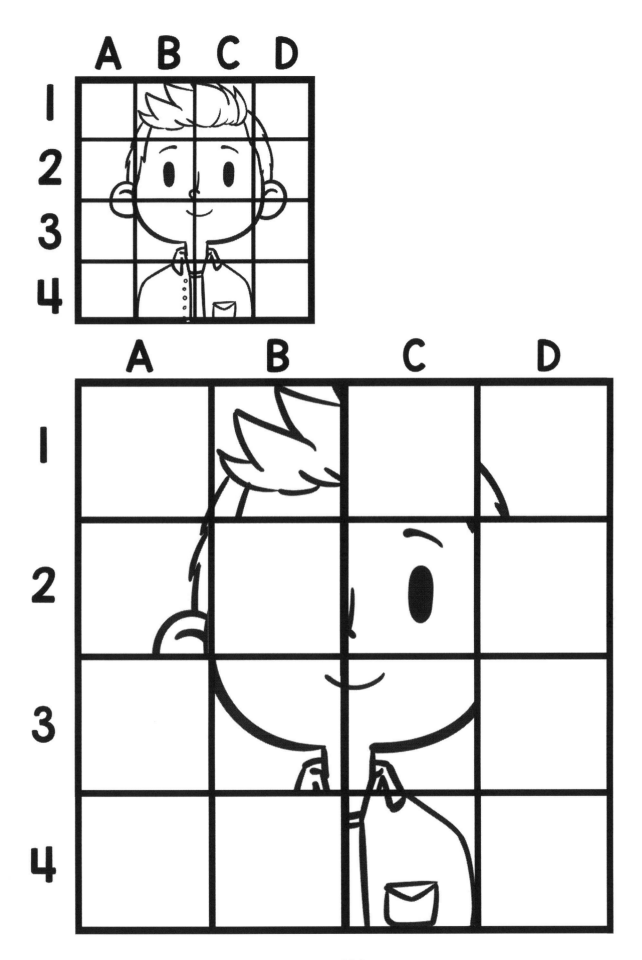

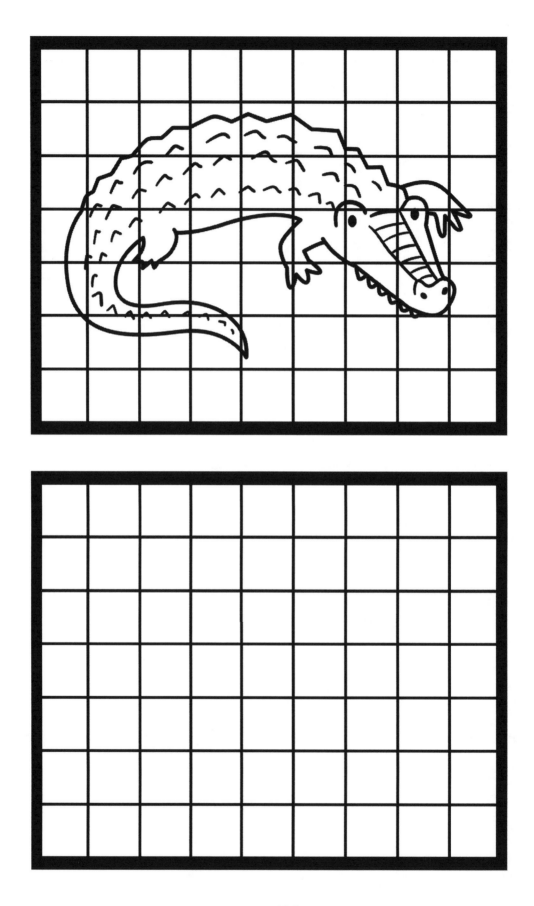

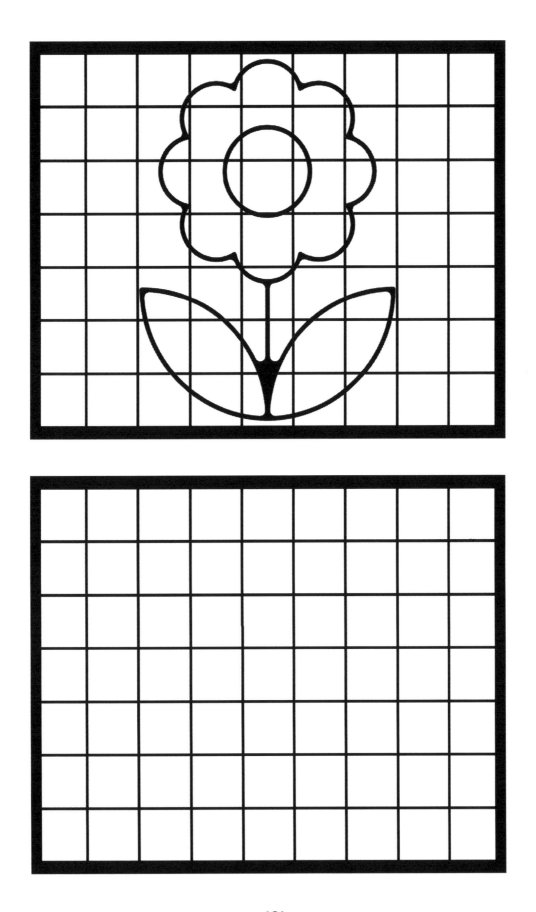

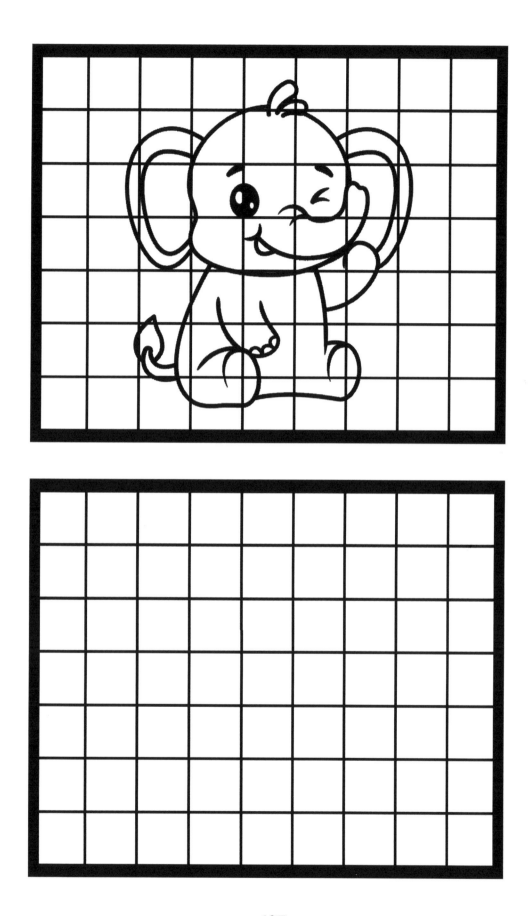

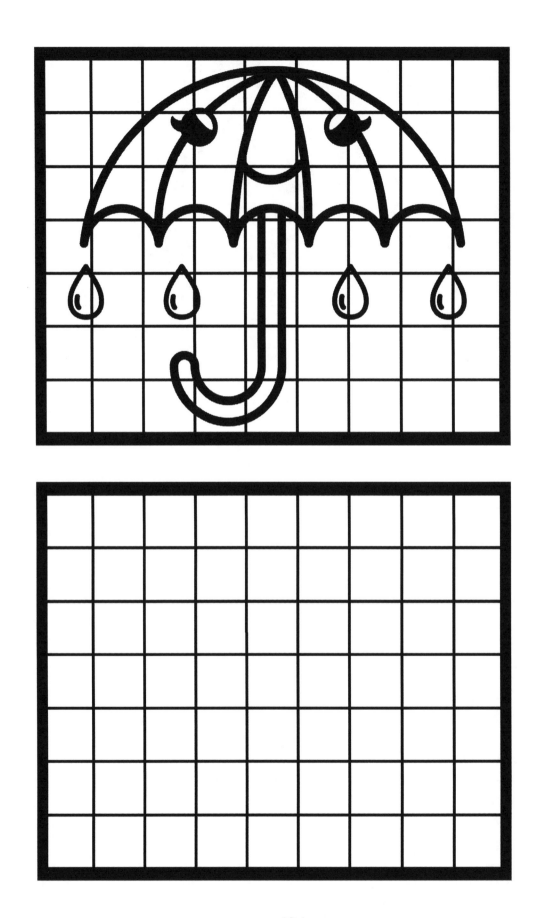

Station 8: Learning to observe

Are you ready to learn some new skills?

You have to look very carefully and observe exactly what's going on to find solutions.

Find the images we are looking for and circle them.

Connect the right parts

Find those that are matching and circle them

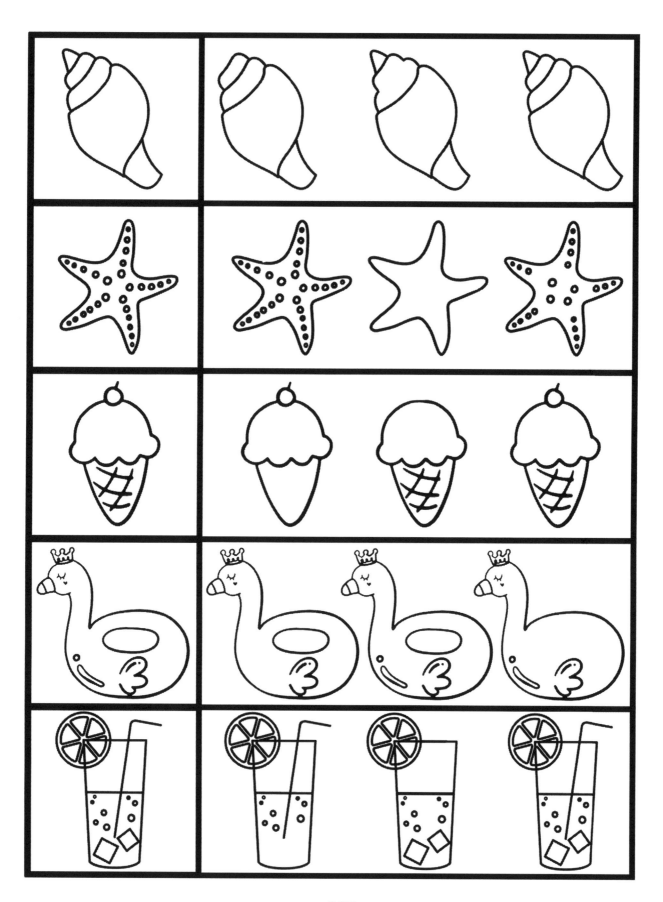

Station 9: Learning to solve riddles

It's going to be exciting again.

At the next station you can test all your
knowledge and skills and solve some
fun riddles.

Solve the puzzle and draw the right shapes in the right order.

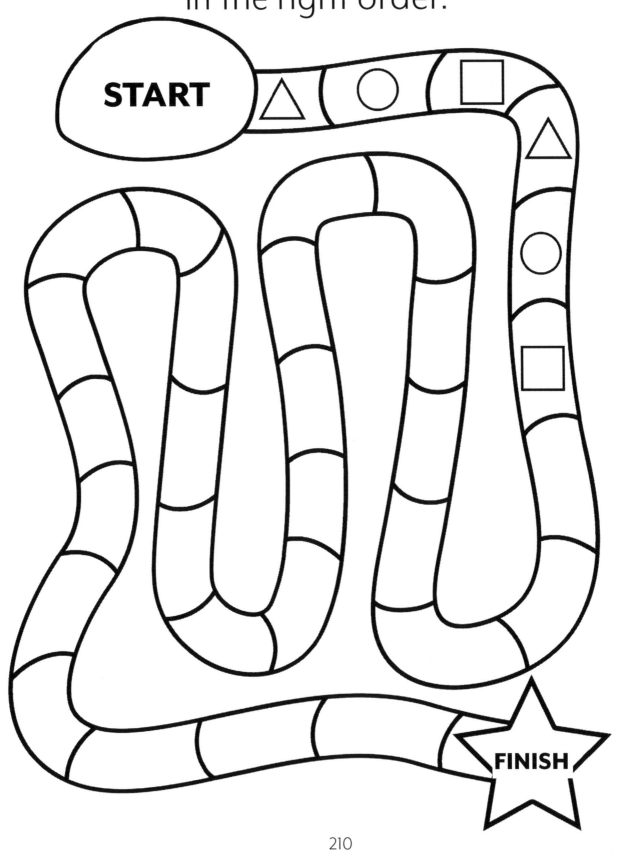

210

What belongs togheter?
Match the correct form.

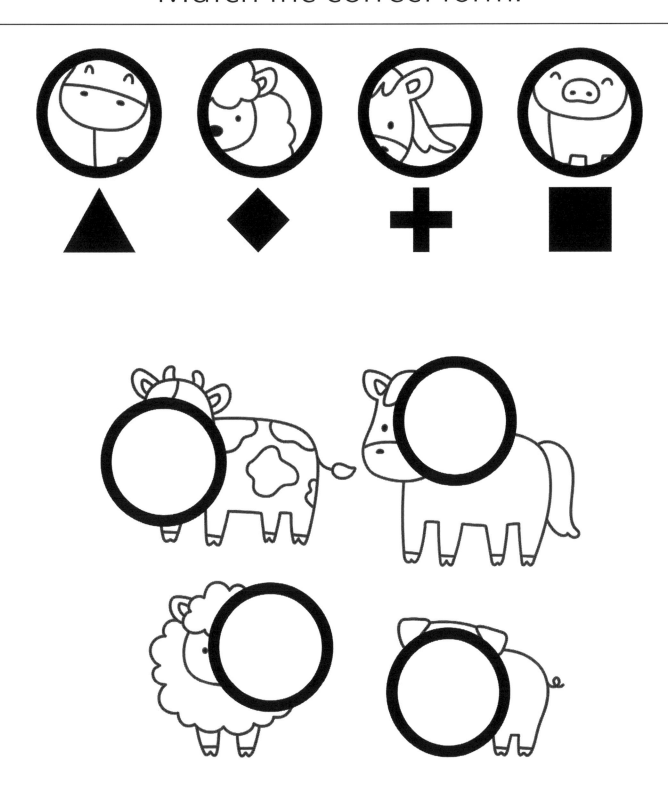

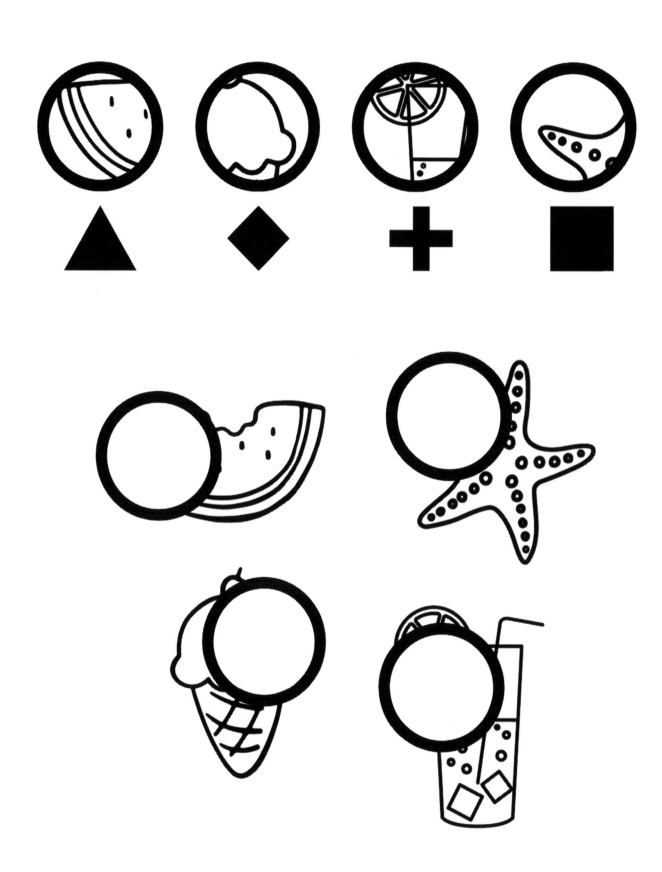

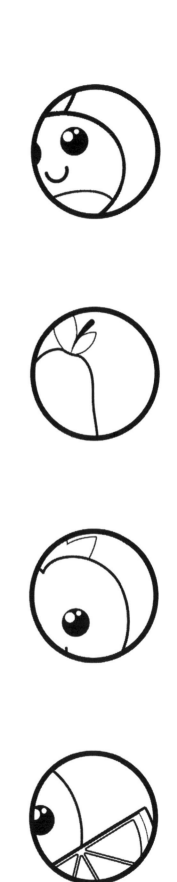

Find the way through the maze and solve it!

FINISH

START

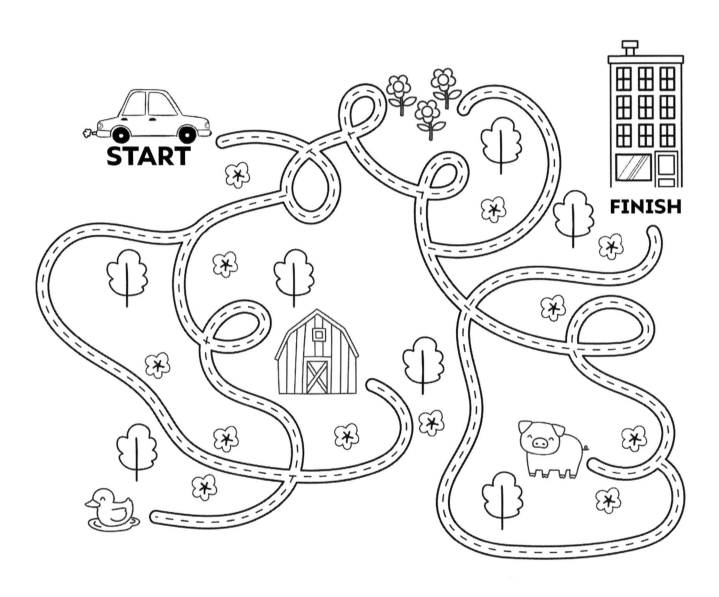

START

FINISH

Find the right shadow!

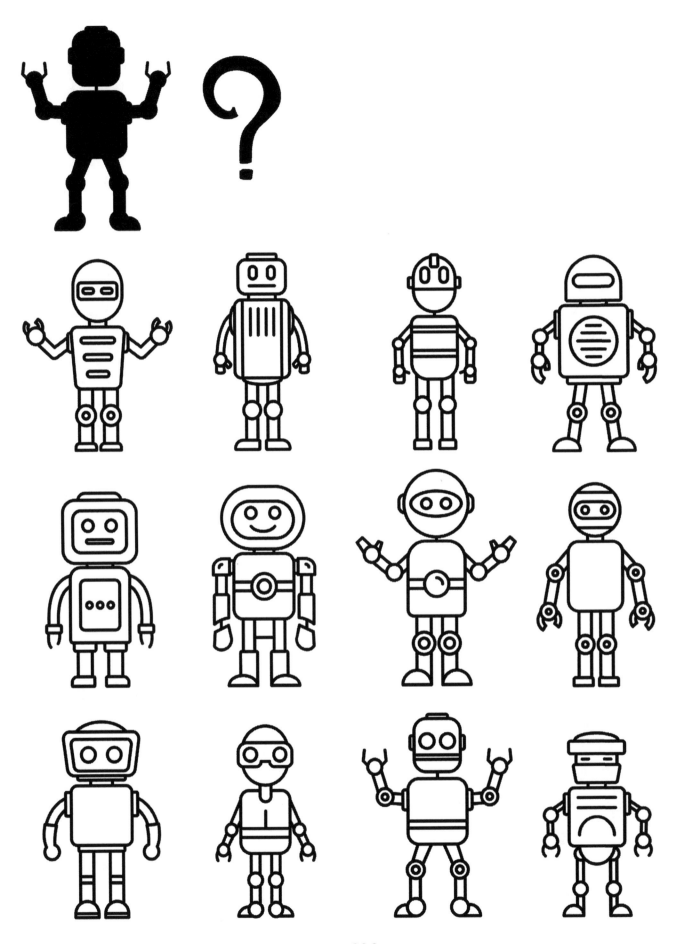

230

Combine correctly!

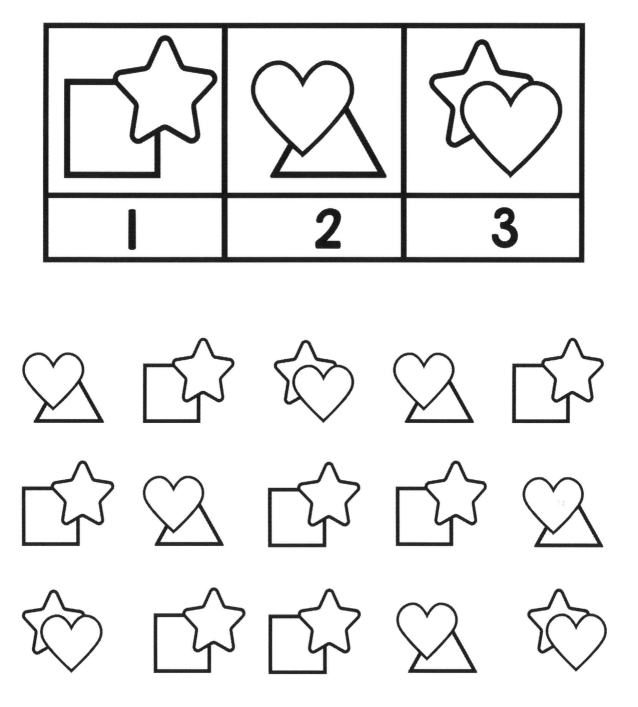

Which form is correct? Circle it.

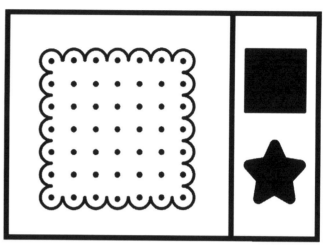

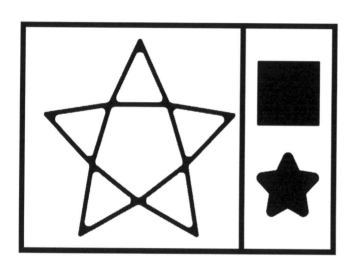

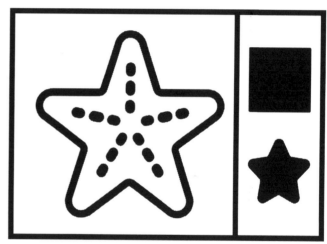

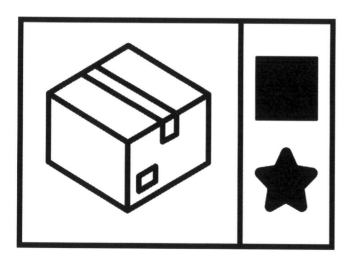

How does the sequence continue?

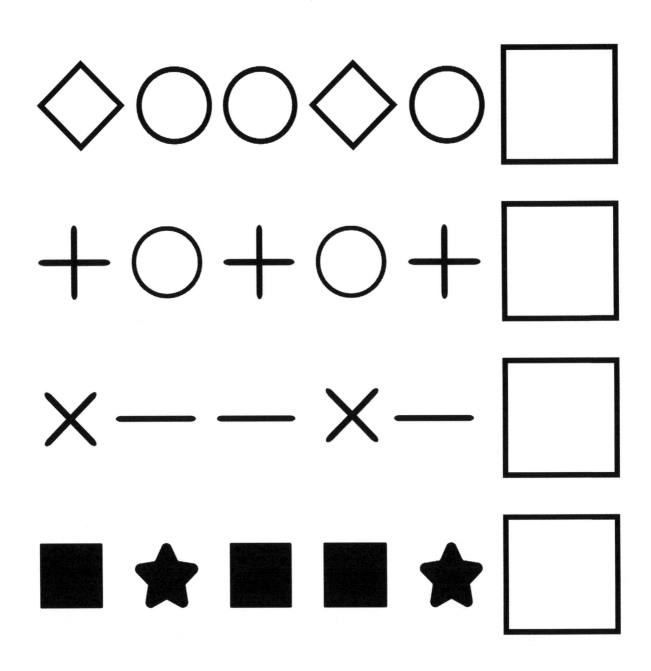

234

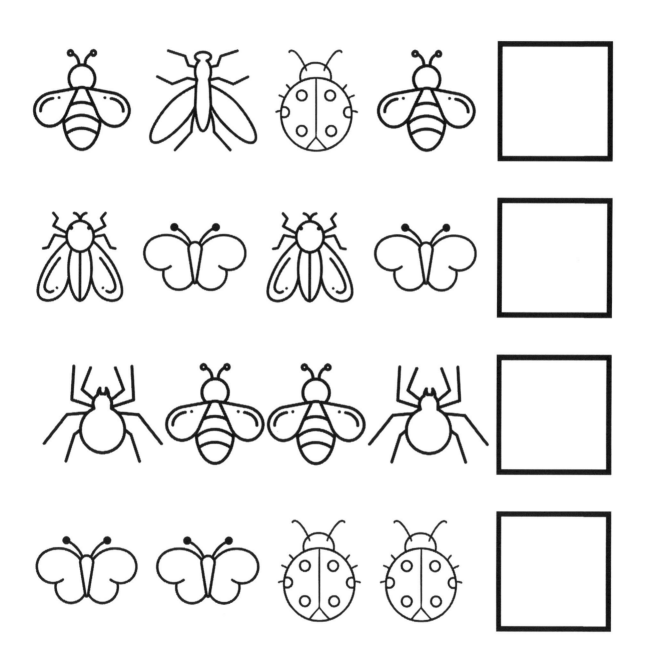

What weighs more? Draw in the boxes.

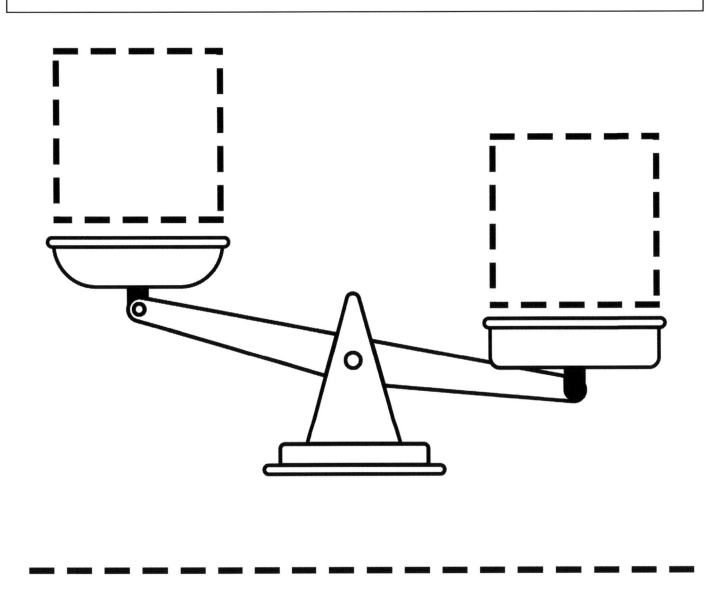

BONUS: Italian words

Regalo

cat = gatto

dog = cane

bird = uccello

rabbit = coniglio

cow = mucca

elephant = elefante

mom = mamma

dad = papá

brother = fratello

sister = sorella

grandmother = nonna

grandfather = nonno

spring = primavera

summer = estate

autumn = autunno

winter = inverno

BONUS: German words

Geschenk

Katze --- = cat

Hund --- = dog

Vogel --- = bird

Kaninchen = rabbit

Kuh --- = cow

Elefant - = elephant

Mutter = mother

Vater = father

Bruder = brother

Schwester = sister

Großmutter = granny

Großvater = grandpa

Frühling = spring

Sommer = summer

Herbst = autumn

Winter = winter

DIPLOMA
OF COMPLETION

IT IS CERTIFIED THAT

_____

IS READY TO START THE FIRST GRADE OF ELEMENTARY SCHOOL

DATE

Did you like this book and did it meet your expectations?
If you are happy with your purchase and brought joy to your child, I would be very
happy to receive a review on Amazon.

Feedback and reviews on Amazon are very important to me and my work as an author and educator. On the one hand I get feedback, I know what is well received and what is not.
On the other hand reviews help all the other customers too.

Just log into your Amazon account,select this book and let me know what you and your child think about it. With a little effort you would help me and all my other customers tremendously.
Thank you!

Abby Lyon

EXCLUSION
OF RESPONSIBILITY

COPYRIGHT

Imprint:
© Abby Lyon
2021

1. Edition

Contact: Thomas Larch/Platt 132/39013 Moso in Val Passiria/Italy
E-Mail: support@tg48.de

Made in the USA
Columbia, SC
06 May 2025

57602364R00137